UNDER

Understanding
Caste

From Buddha to Ambedkar and Beyond

Second Edition

GAIL OMVEDT

Orient BlackSwan

ORIENT BLACKSWAN PRIVATE LIMITED

Registered Office
3-6-752 Himayatnagar, Hyderabad 500 029 (Telangana), INDIA
e-mail: centraloffice@orientblackswan.com

Other Offices
Bengaluru, Bhopal, Chennai, Ernakulam, Guwahati,
Hyderabad, Jaipur, Kolkata, Lucknow, Mumbai,
New Delhi, Noida, Patna, Vijayawada

ISBN: 978 81 250 4175 7

Typeset by
Le Studio Graphique, Gurgaon 122 001
in Bembo 11/13

Printed at
Glorious Printers
Delhi

Published by
Orient Blackswan Private Limited
1/24 Asaf Ali Road, New Delhi 110 002
e-mail: delhi@orientblackswan.com

CONTENTS

Introduction

For most people, even scholars, 'Hinduism' has been a taken-for-granted concept. Hindus are the people of India. Hinduism is their religion. Beginning with the *Ṛg Veda* to the philosophers and even contemporary political leaders, it has been seen as a unique phenomenon of spirituality linked to a practical life; and with a solid geographical base in a diversified subcontinent. Although its stability has been broken from time to time by invasions, conquests and disturbances, it has nevertheless maintained a fair continuity. It has given birth to rampant and unjustifiable social inequalities but has also spawned the protests against these. Its greatest virtue has been its elasticity, its pluralism, its lack of dogma. Hinduism, it is said, has no 'orthodoxy' (though it may have an 'orthopraxy'). With a core in the religious tradition going back to the Vedas and Upanishads, it has brought forth other sister/child religions—Jainism, Buddhism, Sikhism—all born out of the same fertile continuate of tradition, all part of India and Hinduism's contributions to the world.

This image, encompassing the cultural diversities of the subcontinent and subordinating them to a *Vedantic* core, has pervaded both popular and scholarly writings on India. To take but one example, two scholars of 'religion in Maharashtra' draw together dalit, Marxist and *bhakti* traditions in a book entitled *The Experience of Hinduism*, only to give *Vedantam* the last word:

> Buddhists, Jains, Muslims, Christians, nay even the Marxists, of today's India cannot help partaking of it—they are all Hindu-Bharatiya at

heart.... What is it to be a Hindu-Bharatiya? What does it involve? Chiefly, the accepting of the other world as well as this world, the attempt to reconcile the two. But between the two the other world comes first. Brahman and maya are both real, but brahman is the ultimate reality.... This ultimate/provisional duality has been resolved into a unity in the Vedanta of nonduality. (Bhave 1988, 318–19)

There are many who would contest this violently, and as we shall see the Indian tradition is much more than 'Hinduism' so defined. What is more striking, though, is that behind the image of flexibility and diversity is a hard core of an assertion of dominance. "Between the two the other world comes first"—this assertion leads to the political line of the Vishwa Hindu Parishad (VHP) that there may be various versions of what is defined as the 'Hindu tradition' (Sikhism, Buddhism, Jainism, Arya Samaj and Sanatan dharma are the ones usually mentioned), but there is no question that the core is 'traditional' Hinduism—what is known, somewhat fallaciously, as *sanatan dharma*.

Out of the pleasantries of the official ideology of Hindu pluralism and tolerance and under the pressures of contemporary material deprivation and economic turbulence, has grown the modern politics of *Hindutva*—militant Hinduism, Hinduism as nationalism. It makes a simple addition to the claim that Hinduism is the main religion of the people of India: Hinduism is the national religion, the people's tradition in the subcontinent, but it has been attacked, smothered, insulted, dishonoured, first by Muslim aggressors, then by British colonialism, and now by the contemporary State which in its self-definition as "secular" is dishonouring it in its own land and pampering Muslim and Christian minorities. Hinduism's great virtue was its generous tolerance of other faiths, but its enemies have taken advantage of this; Hindus must now be strong, fierce and proud, and not hesitate to assert themselves.

Today, large sections of left and democratic forces and all new social movements are trying to argue and organise against the growing influence of Hindutva or Hindu-nationalism. The majority of these have taken a position against 'communalism' but not against 'Hinduism' as such. The 'secular' version of this opposition argues that Indians must come together beyond their religious identities, as citizens of a nation and as human beings. It is exemplified in the popular anti-communal song *Mandir-Masjid*:

In temples, mosques, gurudwaras
God is divided.
Divide the earth, divide the sea,
But don't divide humanity.
The Hindu says, 'The temple is mine,
The temple is my home.'
The Muslim says, 'Mecca is mine,
Mecca is my loyalty.'
The two fight, fight and die,
Get finished off in fighting...

The song goes on to describe the machinations of political leaders and the perpetuation of exploitation through communalism, but interestingly enough, even its appeal to a common identity draws on (and reproduces?) the notion that India is the home of the Hindus, while the Muslims find their loyalties elsewhere.

An even more eloquent version can be found in Kabir,

The Hindu says Ram is dear,
The Muslim says Rahiman
They quarrel, fight and kill each other
Never knowing the essence.

Another mode of opposing communalism is to re-appeal to Hindu traditions themselves, a position that has been developing among several anti-communal Delhi intellectuals over the last few years. This has been eloquently voiced by Madhu Kishwar in a number of *Manushi* articles which argue 'in defence of our dharma'. Agreeing with the condemnation that Nehruvian and modern left secularism are insufficient to deal with the need for identity, she appeals to bhakti traditions as the 'true Hinduism', and argues that the militaristic image of Rama is a distortion, and that much of casteism is in fact a colonial heritage. This position has antagonised many secular feminists, but there is no denying that it is persuasive to many, particularly to middle-class, upper-caste Indians. Even the upper-caste left is being increasingly drawn to it. This is illustrated by the poster of the Sampradayikta Virodhi Abhyan (SVM): the mask of Rama, the form of Ravana. The SVM thus appeals to the 'gentle' image of Rama and takes for granted the demonical quality of Ravana.

These two forms of opposition to Hindutva—the 'secular' and 'Hindu reformist' versions—draw respectively upon Nehruvian and Gandhian traditions. While there is no reason to doubt the genuineness of their attempts to oppose the aggressive politics of the Hindutva forces, what is questionable is that they accept the validity of the general identification of 'Hindu' with 'Bharatiya', of Hinduism with the tradition of India.

It is necessary to go beyond this debate which poses 'secularism' or a 'reformed Hinduism' as the alternative to Hindutva. This means going beyond 'Hinduism' itself.

Beyond this debate between the secularists and the Hindu reformists there are many voices in India today which not only query the BJP (Bharatiya Janata Party)/VHP interpretation of Hinduism, but also contest the very existence of Hinduism as a primordial force in India. A Tamil dalit scholar-activist, Guna, writes:

> The very concept of Hinduism, which took shape in the north only when the Muslim rule was being consolidated ... was never known to the Tamils until the period of British colonization.... The Brahmans, who had English education and had the opportunity of studying abroad, took some threads from the Europeans who conceived of a political entity called 'Hindustan'. With the borrowed idea, they could clumsily merge the divergent cults and Brahmanic caste apartheid to term it as Hinduism. This concept ... resulted in formulating a pseudo-religious-political concept called 'Hinduism', based on which they sought to define their myth of a 'Hindu' nationhood.... The 'Hindu' was thus born just two centuries back; and he is still a colourless, odourless and formless illusory artificial construction. (Guna 1984, 124–25)

Guna is part of a broader tradition or set of traditions which have put forth alternative interpretations of Indian identity (or identities). These have been socially based among the lower castes, dalits and non-Brahmans, drawing on peasant (and women's) traditions, mainly in the southern, western and outlying regions of the subcontinent. In contemporary times they draw on such leaders as Phule, Ambedkar, Periyar; they appeal to heroes of revolt such as Birsa Munda and Veer Narayan Singh; they claim the traditions of Buddha and Carvak, Mahavir, Kabir, Guru Nanak and Basavappa; they claim heroes like Shivaji but contest the Hinduist interpretation of him; they claim the glories of Mohenjo-daro and the heritage of the pre-state tribals as opposed to that of plundering Aryan tribes. In contrast to the secularist opposition to Hindutva, they proclaim a new politics of a radically transformed non-Hindu identity, and in contrast to reformist Hindu identities *they define 'Hinduism' itself as an oppressive class/caste/patriarchal force.*

The dalit movement, based on ex-untouchables and widening to include non-brahman castes of many southern and peripheral areas, has in recent times brought forward most strongly this ideological challenge, this contesting of Hinduism. Indeed the impetus to challenge the hegemony and validity of Hinduism is part of the very logic of dalit politics.

Dalit politics, the dalit vision, in fact, requires going beyond even the term 'dalit'. In the last decades this has become the most widely accepted word for the most oppressed and exploited sections of the caste system. But others—the 'other backward castes', the former shudras, the 'non-Brahmans' generally—have been also oppressed and exploited within the 'graded hierarchy' which Ambedkar had called caste. They have also contributed to the fight against it. Some of the most profound expressions of a 'dalit vision' have come from those who were not strictly 'dalit' themselves—people like Phule, Periyar, Kabir, Tukaram—even, for that matter, Buddha himself, who represents the starting point of a long journey towards social equality and social justice.

It is insufficient to see dalit politics as simply the challenge posed by militant organisations such as the Dalit Panthers, the factionalised Republican Party, the rallies of the Bahujan Samaj Party (BSP), or even the insurgencies carried out by low-caste based Naxalite organisations. Dalit politics as the challenge to brahman hegemony took on wider forms throughout the 1970s and 1980s, its themes sweeping into movements of 'backward castes' (the former shudras of the traditional *varna* system), peasants, women, and tribals. Dalit politics in the sense of a challenge to brahmanic tradition has been an aspect of 'several new social movements'. Strikingly, if we take 1972, the year of the founding of the Dalit Panthers, as a year from when began a new phase of the dalit movement, it was also a crucial year for many other new social movements—from the founding of the Self Employed Women's Association (SEWA) in Ahmedabad to the upsurge of a new environmental movement in the Tehri-Garhwal Himalayan foothills, from the agitations and organisations of farmers in Punjab and Tamil Nadu, to the rise of tribal-based movements for autonomy in the central Indian region of Jharkhand. These movements though not as directly as the dalit movement, came to contest the way in which the Hindu-nationalist forces sought to depict and hegemonise Indian culture. They often linked a cultural critique to a broader critique of socio-economic development and an opposition to the over-centralised political system. By the late 1980s, an intermixing and dialogue of all these themes could be seen. The events of 1989–1991 ended with a setback resulting in the renewed aggressiveness of the forces of Hindu nationalism—but we continue to hope that the setback has been temporary.

One

Two Great Traditions of India and the Construction of Hinduism

Is 'Hinduism' only a construction, and a recent one at that? In a sense all nationalisms and identities are constructions. It also seems accurate to say that the identification of the Indian subcontinent with a single people whose religion is Hinduism was only made in recent history, and only in recent decades has it been projected as a national religion centring on *Rama*.

The term *Hindu* is ancient, deriving from Sindhu, the river Indus. The Hindu religion as it is described today is said to have its roots in the Vedas, the poems of the Indo-Europeans whose incursions into the subcontinent took place many centuries after the earliest urban civilisation in India, the Indus civilisation. With the script—if it is that—still undeciphered, little is known about the heart of this civilisation; it was widespread, impressive, relatively equalitarian, lacking weapons of war, and has left us only a few statuary relics, including a beautiful fragile dancing girl and an authoritative, bearded male, possibly a priest.

Most archaeologists today doubt that the 'Aryans' were the main force responsible for the destruction of this civilisation, but it seems fairly clear that many of their early poems celebrated its downfall, with the rain god Indra claiming to be the 'destroyer of cities' and the 'releaser of waters'. In any case, whatever we call the religion of these nomadic clans, it was not the religion that is today known as

Hinduism. This began to be formulated only in the period of the founding of the Magadha-Mauryan state in the period ranging from the Upanishads and the formation of Vedantic thought to the consolidation of the social order represented by the *Manusmriti*. But it was then known as brahmanism, and Buddhism and Jainism (as well as the materialist Carvak tradition) are equally old. Both Buddhism and Jainism claim that they can trace their heritage back to Mohenjo-daro; with the Buddha and Mahavir being only the last in a long line of teachers. Brahmanic Hinduism, as we know it, in other words, arose out of only one of many consolidations within a diverse subcontinental cultural tradition. In its form of brahmanism, reworked and absorbing many indigenous traditions, it attained social and political hegemony only during the sixth to tenth century, often after violent confrontations with Buddhism and Jainism.

It was in this period that the subcontinent as a territory came to be known throughout the world as 'Hindustan' or 'Al-Hind' in Arabic. But this did not refer to religion and the Muslim rulers of the land were also known as Hindustanis. The major strands within what was later to be called Hinduism were known separately in the south as Shaivism and Vaishnavism, and their influence spread throughout south-east Asia as separate traditions.

The main themes of brahmanic Hinduism were the identification of orthodoxy with acceptance of the authority of the Vedas and the Brahmans and the idea of *varnashrama dharma*—the fourfold system of castes and stages of life—as the ideal social structure. *Advaita*, the identification of a 'self' or *atman* within each individual with the universal 'brahman' was the favoured philosophy. As it developed, brahmanism had a tremendous absorptive and co-optive power as long as dissident elements accepted their place within a caste hierarchy. The material base of this social order lay in the village productive system of caste, *jajmani* and untouchability.

Nevertheless it is doubtful whether the masses of the people at this time identified themselves as Hindus. There were numerous local gods and goddesses who remain the centre of popular religious life even today; and the period gave birth to bhakti or devotional cults (sometimes centred on non-Vedic gods such as

Vithala in Maharashtra) which rebelled against caste hierarchy and brahman domination. Many of these in turn developed into religious traditions that consider themselves explicitly non-Hindu (Sikhism, Veerasaivism, etc.).

It was, in fact, only the colonial period which saw a consolidation of the identification of India or Hindustan (the land) and the people who inhabited it, with a particular religion known as Hinduism, interpreted as being the primal and ancient religion of the subcontinent. This was the construction of Hinduism. The Europeans, with their racism, romanticism, fascination with the Vedas and Orientalism, played an important role in this. But the major work of constructing Hinduism was done by the Indian elites. In the nineteenth century, people like Lokmanya Tilak adopted the 'Aryan theory of race', claimed a white racial stock for upper-caste Indians and accepted the Vedas as their core literature. Tilak was also the first to try and unite a large section of the masses around brahmanical leadership, with the public celebration of the Ganesh festival. Anti-Muslim themes underlay the construction of Shivaji as the founder of a 'Hindu *raj*', a process, which was incidentally ideologically contested even in the nineteenth century (see O'Hanlon 1988). By the end of the century, Hindu conservatives were mounting a full-scale attack on their upper-caste reformist rivals with charges that the latter were 'anti-national', and succeeded in excluding the Social Reform Conference from any coordinated meetings with the National Congress.

Significant developments took place in the 1920s with the founding of the Rashtriya Swayamsevak Sangh (RSS) by Hegdewar and the Hindu Mahasabha by Savarkar. Savarkar was the first to proclaim a full-scale Hindu nationalism or Hindutva, linking race, blood and territory. He proclaimed himself an atheist and his theory laid less emphasis on religion as such; yet his Sanskritic, Aryan interpretation was clear: he disliked any idea of mixing Hindi and Urdu, refused to admit the linguistic/cultural diversity of India, and was consistently anti-Muslim in his politics.

Tilak and Savarkar were Maharashtrian Chitpavan brahmans, the caste which comprised rulers displaced from power in western India by the British. The Chitpavans were already under pressure from a strong non-brahman and dalit movement by the 1920s. Significantly, the claim to an Aryan racial heritage was given a major reinterpretation in the 1930s, clearly under pressure from the non-brahman movement's reversal of it: Aryanism and the notion of a Vedic, Sanskritic core to Hinduism was not given up, but it began to be argued by ideologues like Golwalkar, that the Aryans themselves had had their original home in the Indian subcontinent (see Pandey 1991;Yechury 1993).

Nevertheless, Hindu nationalism found its strongest base in north India, the place where the emotive slogan 'Hindi-Hindu-Hindustan' made the most sense. Here, the previous empire had been controlled by Muslims and there were still a large number of Muslims from all social sections. Thus, beneath the ideological formulation of 'Hinduism as nationalism' was a growing identification with religious community. Peasants, artisans and others identified themselves in religious terms, with 'Hindu' and 'Muslim' communities emerging as independent entities out of what had been a fairly deep linguistic-cultural synthesis, in a process which Gyan Pandey has described as "the construction of communalism in north India." Both groups not only formulated their identities in religious terms but called for political power to protect them. As Pandey describes the process, "the idea of a Hindu raj which would reflect the glories of the ancient Hindu civilization and keep Muslims in their place" was "matched in due course by the notion of a Muslim Raj which would protect the place of the Muslims" (Pandey 1990, 235). These tensions gradually led to efforts at organising an identity at the national level.

Once it was accepted that two separate communities, Hindus and Muslims, existed at an all-India level, there were only two possible courses for creating an overriding national identity. One was taken by Gandhi, the other by Nehru and the leftists. The Gandhian solution involved taking India as a coalition of communities, each maintaining its identity but uniting by unfolding the wealth of tolerance and love which lay in each religious tradition; the Nehruvian solution consisted of forging a secular identity on the basis of modernity and socialism that transcended, and in the process rejected, separate religious communal identities.

Gandhi's solution rested on a deep recognition of the importance of popular traditions; indeed throughout most of his political life his ability to draw upon such traditions helped make him the most important mass leader of his time and in formulating an ideal of development that was different from the centralised industrial path later followed. Gandhi identified himself as a Hindu, but gave his own, sometimes breathtaking, interpretations of what it meant to be a Hindu. "The *Vedas, Upanishads, Smritis* and *Puranas* including the Ramayana and the Mahabharata are Hindu scriptures," he notes, but then insists on his right to interpret. He rejects anything that does not fit his idea of spirituality: "Nothing can be accepted as the word of God which cannot be tested by reason or be capable of being spontaneously experienced" (Gandhi's reply to Ambedkar's 'Annihilation of Caste' in *The Harijan*—in Ambedkar 1979, 82). But inevitably this very acceptance of the Hindu identity meant an absorbing of the caste element of this identity:

> Caste has nothing to do with religion… it is harmful to both spiritual and natural growth. *Varna* and *Ashrama* are institutions which have nothing to do with castes. The law of *Varna* teaches us that we have each one of us to earn our bread by following the ancestral calling … The calling of a Brahman—a spiritual teacher—and of a scavenger are equal and their due performance carries equal merit before God and at one time seems to have carried identical reward before man. (Quoted in Ambedkar 1979, 83)

This was a formulation that accepted a hereditary place or calling for a human being and would obviously be rejected by militant low castes.

Gandhi's social reformism as well as his proposed developmental path, a kind of 'green' projection of a sustainable, decentralised society that grew out of a powerful critique of industrial society, were in the end tied to a Hinduism that accepted a brahmanic core: the limitations of needs in which both technology and sexuality were seen as tying humans down to desire (*maya*), and in which the guiding role of intellectuals was accepted. '*Ram raj*' made Gandhi ultimately not simply a Hindu but also an indirect spokesman for upper-caste interests.

Not surprisingly, Gandhi had his biggest aspirations, confrontations, and failures on the issue of caste. His clash with Ambedkar at the time of the Second Round Table Conference (the second of the two conferences called by the British at the beginnings of the 1930s to have a negotiated settlement regarding the political shape of India) showed that he put his identity as a Hindu before that as a national leader (see Omvedt 1994, chapter 5). Many of the lower castes were in the end alienated from Gandhi's version of anti-communal Hinduism, notwithstanding his courage, or his murder at the hands of militant Hinduism itself. Ambedkar's judgement—"this Gandhi age is the dark age of Indian politics. It is an age in which people instead of looking for their ideals in the future are returning to antiquity"—was harsh, but expressed the dalit choice of modernity over the Hindu version of tradition.

But the other alternative, Nehruvian secularism, had its own problems. Like Gandhi, Nehru took the existence of a Hindu identity for granted. In contrast to Gandhi, his idea of building a modern India was to ignore religious identity, seeing it as ultimately irrelevant or of secondary importance in the modern world. Leftists and Nehruvian socialists alike took class as the ultimate reality at the social level, and sought to transcend this with an abstract nationalism, seeing all communal/religious identities as feudal. They believed that economic and technological development would make such identities redundant. Nehru's (and the left's) secularism thus seems indissoluble from a naive faith in industrial/scientific progress:

> In my opinion, a real solution will only come when economic issues, affecting all religious groups and cutting across communal boundaries, arise.... I am afraid I cannot get excited over this communal issue, important as it is temporarily. It is after all a side issue, and it can have no real importance in the larger scheme of things. (Nehru 1941, 410–11)

Nehru's secularism, as much as Gandhi's self-professed Hinduism, was underpinned by Hinduist assumptions about Indian society and history, although he expressed, throughout his writings, a full appreciation of plurality and diversity. He says again and again that India is not to be identified with Hinduism, that Buddhism is a separate religion, that caste is to be condemned. And yet the broad framework of his thinking saw brahmanic Hinduism as the 'national' religion, setting the framework within which other traditions could be absorbed:

> Previously, in the ages since the Aryans had come down to what they called Aryavarta or Bharatvarsha, the problem that faced India was to produce a synthesis between this new race and culture and the old race and civilization of the land. To that the mind of India devoted itself and it produced an enduring solution built on the strong foundations of a joint Indo-Aryan culture. Other foreign elements came and were absorbed ... That mixture of religion and philosophy, history and tradition, custom and social structure, which in its wide fold included almost every aspect of India and which might be called Brahmanism or (to use a later word) Hinduism, became the symbol of nationalism. It was indeed a national religion, with its appeal to all those deep instincts, racial and cultural, which form the basis everywhere of nationalism today. (Nehru 1982, 138)

This had disturbing elements in common with the Hindutva discourse. Along with this, while Nehru condemned caste wholeheartedly, he disliked any intrusion of it into politics; he thought that demands (such as reservations) raised by non-brahman and dalit groups were divisive, and tried to ignore them. His historical discussion of caste sees it as essentially functionalist and integrative; it is clear that whatever the superficial influence of Marxism, his view of Indian society did not genuinely encompass a sense of exploitation and contradiction:

> Thus caste was a group system based on services and functions. It was meant to be an all-inclusive order without any common dogma and allowing the fullest latitude to each group....The organization of society being, generally speaking, competitive and nonacquisitive, these divisions into castes did not make as much difference as they might otherwise have done. The Brahmin at the top, proud of his intellect and learning and respected by others, seldom had much in the way of worldly possessions.... *Mythical?*

Merchants, he argues, had no high standing, the vast majority of the population were agriculturalists with rights to the land who gave only a sixth share to the king or state: "Thus in a sense, every group from the state to the scavenger was a shareholder in the produce" (Ibid., 252–53).

Nehru's secularism then, shows the degree to which the 'construction of Hinduism' in the late nineteenth and early twentieth century had succeeded in making a brahmanical interpretation of Indian social history hegemonic, not only for those who militantly identified as Hindus but for those who prided themselves on avoiding such an identification. In ignoring the challenge of the anti-caste radicals, in failing to deconstruct the actual meaning of such constructions as 'Hindu culture', the Indian left and progressive elites allowed the maintenance of brahmanic assumptions of superiority and authority, the right of the elites to rule, and to assume the role of guardians. Nehruvian assumptions which saw communal harmony or 'secularism' as achieved from above by a powerful state fit in easily with the statism that was to mark India's version of industrial development. As Pandey puts it,

> By the 1930s and 1940s, the importance of an 'enlightened' leadership was thus being stressed on all sides as the critical ingredient that was required in the bid to advance the 'backward' peoples.... It had taken great leaders, a Chandragupta Maurya, an Ashoka, an Akbar, to actualize the dreams of Indian unity in the past and they had done so in the great states and empires that they had established. It would take great leaders like Nehru and Patel to realize the newly created unity of India, and the state would again be their major instrument. The twentieth century liberal ... could do no better than to turn to statism. (Pandey 1990, 253–54)

What the 'construction of Hinduism' successfully accomplished was to establish Hinduism as a taken-for-granted religion of the 'majority' linked to the backward peasant core of a pre-industrial society. In this context Gandhi identified with it, and with the peasantry as he understood it; Nehru saw both as backward and inferior. Both accepted the brahmanic core of Hinduism and the need for a paternalistic enlightened leadership. Both responses ultimately failed—in overcoming a 'Hindu' identity, in reforming it sufficiently to allow a full participation in its religious centre by the low castes and in preventing the growth of a virulent and aggressive form of the religion, interpreting it as the national identity of India. By the 1990s both Gandhism and Nehruism were reeling under the blows of popular disillusionment and the rise of the most hostile forms of 'Hindu nationalism'.

Right from the outset, though, a more fundamental challenge to Hinduism was taking shape. It took shape during the colonial period pioneered by the theories and polemics of a shudra (peasant) caste social radical from western India, Jotiba Phule. But it had its roots long before that, in the long traditions of dalit-bahujan based equalitarian traditions beginning with Buddha and the *shramanas*. Let us then begin with a historical look, at the other 'Great Tradition' of India that had its origin 'before Hinduism'.

Two

Before Hinduism
The Buddhist Vision

> Monks, All is aflame. What All is aflame? The eye is aflame. Forms
> are aflame. Consciousness at the eye is aflame. Contact at the eye is
> aflame. And whatever there is that arises in dependence on contact
> at the eye—experienced in pleasure, pain, or neither-pleasure-nor-
> pain—that too is aflame. Aflame with what? Aflame with the fire
> of passion, the fire of aversion, the fire of delusion. Aflame, I tell
> you, with birth, aging and death, with sorrows, lamentations, pains,
> distresses, and despairs....
>
> Translation by Thanissaro Bhikku
> (See Upreti 1997, 112)

So went the famous 'fire sermon' of Buddha. His emphasis of
course was on the spiritual condition of human beings; it was
psychological—the enemy was desire and grasping. But it was also
a metaphor for his times. In the middle of the first millennium
BCE, society was caught in the fires of profound change. Iron and
other inventions had increased agricultural production. Trade
and commerce were on the rise. Cities were growing, and new
kingdoms—particularly Magadha and Kosala in what is now
Bihar—were appearing as new political forms challenging the
older, semi-tribal oligarchic republics. People were caught in
the throes of change, commercialisation and the growing class

society. *Dasa-kammakaras* (slaves/workers) provided the surplus, with artisan guilds also flourishing and many rich merchants and landowners. And the two major streams of thought—brahmanic and shramanic—were contending.

The brahmanic stream had its philosophical side, based largely among forest recluses, and its ritual side, found among the intellectual advisors of the rising kings. Buddhists and other shramana trends also had their spiritual foundation among those who had renounced all worldly desires but not all of these lived in the forests. Some, as the Buddhist themselves, settled for at least much of the year in monasteries located near the cities. The support for their thinking came from the rising merchant classes and many of the working peasantry. This was true of both Buddhism and Jainism; Jainism, which survived in enclaves much longer became very largely a merchant religion.

Caste was only in an incipient phase at this time, a projection of the brahmanic ideas. Upon being questioned by the young brahman Vasettha, about who is a brahman, one who is born for seven births in a brahman family, or someone who behaves nobly, by birth (*jati*) or by action (*kamma*)—Buddha had replied denying all biological (jati) differences among human beings, and defining a person by what he or she did.

One of the Buddhist *jataka*s (tales) described the contention of the time: the Buddha, born in a Naga (that is probably a trope for a tribal oligarchy) family, is arguing against the theme of a cousin praising brahmanism:

These Vedic studies are the wise man's toils,
The lure which tempts the victims whom he spoils…
'Brahmans he made for study, for command
he made the Khattiyas; Vessas plough the land;
Suddas the servants made to obey the rest;
thus from the first went forth his high behest…'
We see these rules enforced before our eyes,
none but the Brahmans offer sacrifice,
none but the Khattiya exercises sway.
The Vessas plough, the Suddas must obey.
These greedy liars propagate deceit,

and fools believe the fictions they repeat;
he who has eyes can see the sickening sight;
why does not Brahma set his creatures right?
At first there were no women and no men;
'twas mind first brought mankind to light—and then,
though they all started equal in the race,
their various failures made them soon change place
it was no lack of merit in the past,
but present faults which made them first or last.
The Brahman's Veda, Khattiya's policy,
both arbitrary and delusive be,
they blindly grope their way along a road
by some huge inundation overflowed.
(Cowell 1907, Jataka no. 543)

The Buddhist vision of society and the state—as well as its vision
of enlightenment—differed profoundly from the brahmanic, as
this shows. The ruler was expected to be a righteous 'cakkavati'
king, following the wheel of the *dhamma*—providing salaries to
bureaucrats, capital to merchants, seed to farmers and help to the
poor. This was in contrast to the brahmanic ruler, one of whose main
duties was to enforce the law against *varna-samkara*, the mixture of
castes. The Sangha was privileged over the lay community, since it
was the realm where meditation was practiced and enlightenment
was sought; it was not until later, with Mahayana Buddhism, that
it was really conceived that a lay person could attain *nirvana*. But
rather than ritualism, what was encouraged was righteous human
relationships.

In the important *Sigolavada suttanta* in the *Digha Nikaya*[1], the
young merchant Sigola is instructed that rather than follow the
various rituals, he should practice, as part of the 'four quarters', right
relationships with teachers, friends, wives, and dasa-kammakaras
or employees. Then the relations are defined, each one reciprocal.
Employees, or dasa-kammakaras, are to be given a fair wage, leisure
time, a share of luxuries. In return, they would serve their master

---

[1] *Digha Nikaya* or 'Collection of Long Discourses' is a Buddhist scripture,
the first of the five nikayas, or collections, in the Sutta Pitaka, which is one of
the 'three baskets' that compose the Pali Tipitaka of Theravada Buddhism.

joyfully, waking before him, sleeping after, telling his praises. Enterprise was encouraged; gathering wealth without destroying the sources of wealth, as a "honeybee goes from flower to flower". Two parts of the profit were to be re-invested—one saved, one for consumption.

Buddhism was of course unalterably opposed to caste. Not only did he deny it; in many ways the Buddhist texts show a leading role for the 'untouchables' of the time, known as Chandalas. The opposite of the *Vasettha sutta* in the *Sutta Nipatta* is the *Vaselasutta*, which describes the ancient hero Matanga, a glorious spiritual hero before whom nobles and brahmans bowed down. In a jataka his story is elaborated further. The Chandalas are always shown as enemies of brahmans; for instance in one of the stories Sariputta, the Buddha's most esteemed follower, takes birth as a Chandala, and gives true spiritual teaching to a brahman student, forcing him "between his feet" for his inability to answer questions (Cowell 1895, Jataka no. 377). All in all, Buddhism played a leading role in contesting the field of defining social order with brahmanism, and within this gave an important role to untouchables, who are often depicted as spiritual if not quite Buddhist followers.

And the spiritual goal? This was passionlessness, equanimity, freedom from the 'fires' of desire and greed. As verse 251 of the *Dhammapada*[2] put it, "There is no fire like passion, no chains like guilt, no snare like infatuation, no torrent like craving." The ideal is pictured in thousands of Buddha images, peaceful, removed from anguish and pain as well as from great joy. It is not an 'indifferent god', it is not a god of any kind, but a depiction of a goal for every human being. It was a missionary religion; as one of the last instructions of Buddha put it,

> I shall not die, O Evil one! Until the brethren and sisters of the order, and until the lay-disciples of either sex shall have become true hearers, wise and well-trained, ready and learned, versed in the scriptures, fulfilling all the greater and lesser duties, correct in life, walking according to the precepts—until they, having thus

---

[2] A Buddhist scripture containing 423 verses covering essential teachings of the Buddha, spoken by him on various occasions.

themselves learned the doctrine, shall be able to tell others of it, preach it, make it known, establish it, open it, minutely explain it and make it clear—until they, when others start vain doctrine, shall be able by the truth to vanquish and refute it, and so to spread the wonder-working truth abroad! (Mahaparinibanna Sutta, II, 3)[3]

Bahujan sukaya, bahujan hitaya, was the memorable phrase that was used to characterise the social goal of the Buddha: a universal compassion, seeking the welfare of all. And the last words of the Buddha, *atta deepa bhav,* be your own lamp, be your own refuge, characterised the heart of his teachings.

The civilisation that Buddhism helped to create can be seen even today in its stone monuments—caves, sometimes with delicate and sensual paintings, *vihara*s, almost all built on trade routes. It was a civilisation of commerce, one in which India was linked to Greece and Rome on the one hand, and China on the other, with Buddhism and luxury goods flowing along the same routes. The kind of empire that was made possible was shown by the work of Ashoka, his earnest effort to bring morality to the land, his pillars dotting the landscape.

Buddhism was by no means the only 'religion' or teaching; Jainism, Lokayat materialism, the other shramana sects such as the Ajivikas and Shaivism were also prominent. But in many ways it was hegemonic, and shaped the civilisation of early India.

Yet one of the main messages of Buddhism is transience, *anica.* Buddhism proved to be transient in India. Even while the simple morality of the dhamma seemed to underlay a flourishing civilisation, brahmanism was continuing to develop, and in the turmoil of invasions an alliance with kings was formed. Buddhism, even at its height, had never been a 'state religion'; kings may have sponsored it, but pluralism was encouraged. The Sangha held itself aloof from politics, and this was perhaps part of its downfall. By the middle of the first millennium, brahmanism was on the ascendance. Projected first a thousand years before, its own black

---

[3] Mahaparinibanna Sutta, II, 33—translated from the Pali by Sister Vajira and Francis Story; at http://www.accesstoinsight.org/tipitaka/dn/dn.16.1-6.vaji.html, accessed 29 July 2010.

vision of a varnashrama-based society began to triumph, broken only in part by Muslim invasions. Between about the eighth and twelfth century, with the support of brahmanism, a new village society began to form, with the distribution of the surplus based upon jajmani relations, each caste group performing its own 'duty' and able to claim part of the surplus from that. Untouchables began to be condemned to live in special quarters. 'Hinduism' began to take shape, though the name itself was not known.

Resistance however, did not stop. Islam itself bore a message of equality, and though this was muted in the medieval period and its sultans and emperors made common cause with the elite of Indian society, even helped them enforce caste rules, at the lower level the energies of Sufism began to spread, bearing themes of equality and love of god. This and other undercurrents of religious trends among the dalit-bahujan masses began to lay the foundations for a new revolt, with a new vision—that of radical bhakti.

Three

Before Hinduism
The Devotional Visions of Bhakti

They've organized a game on the river sands
The Vaishnavas are dancing, ho!
Pride and wrath they trample underneath their feet,
at one another's feet they're falling, ho!

They dance in thunderous joyousness
singing sacred songs and names, ho!
To the dark ages challenging,
One is stronger than the other, ho! (Refrain)

Sandal paste on foreheads, rosaries and garlands,
they parade themselves with pride, ho!
Cymbals and tabors, a showering of flowers,
an unparalleled festival of joy, ho!

Engrossed in music and entranced
are simple sisters and my brothers, ho!
Pandits, meditators, yogis, Mahanubhavas,
all have won unequalled powers, ho!

Forgotten is the pride of varna and of caste,
each humbling himself before the next, ho!
Minds have become as pure as melted butter,
The stones themselves will melt at last, ho!

Cries of victory reach up to the sky
The Vaishnava heroes feel their power, ho!
Tuka says, you've made an easy road,
To cross the oceans of our life, ho!
(Tukaram 1973, #189)

From the twelfth century onwards new movements expressing the ancient tradition of equality arose in society. The first most clearly datable of these is the Lingayat movement, founded by Basavanna in northern Karnataka. Though he was himself a brahman and a minister in the kingdom of Kalyana, Basava rejected all of this—be it the sacred thread or priestly rituals. Instead he taught a purified form of Saivism, centred around the linga, worn as a personal meditational focus by every person. There were no temples—instead there were areas for free discussion, wandering was emphasised, and both men and women could, as wearers of the linga, perform priestly functions. Basava mocked at the 'idolatry' of those affected by brahmanism and practised a firm monotheism. In fact this was to be true of every radical devotional movement.

> The pot is a god. The winnowing fan is a god. The stone in the street is a god. The comb is a god. The bowstring is also a god. The bushel is a god and the spouted cup is a god. Gods, gods, there are so many there's no place left for a foot. There is only one god. He is our Lord of the Meeting Rivers. (Ramanuja 1973, 84)

Finally, the movement clearly rejected caste and other distinctions,

> What does it mean which background you have?
> He who wears the linga of Siva is well-born!
> Should we inquire about background among the devotees,
> after the castes have been mixed?
> This is the saying:
> Who is born in the caste of Siva's lore, free from rebirth is he;
> Uma his mother, Rudra his sire, and verily the Siva fold his tribe,
> so I will take the leftovers at their place
> and I shall give my daughter to them,

for I believe in your devotees,
O Lord of the Meeting Rivers.
(Shouten 1995, 55)

How strong this was in practice was shown when Basava
sponsored a marriage between the son of a dalit member and the
daughter of a brahman. But, even though he was a minister in the
kingdom, this was too much. The parents were brutally executed;
the result was a near civil war in the kingdom and the Lingayats were
driven out. When the movement revived in the fifteenth century, it
was much more compromising. Few bhakti movements after that
openly—at least—broke the firm caste law of the prohibition of
varna-samkara.

The Tamil radical Siddha movement is less easily datable; its
leading figures appear to be lost in a haze of uncertainty. But there
were strong expressions of resistance to caste and convention:
"Dance, snake, dance!" sang *bhakta*s (devotees, followers) such as
Pambatti Cittar, saying,

> *We'll set fire to divisions of caste*
> *We'll debate philosophical questions in the market place,*
> *We'll have dealings with despised households,*
> *We'll go around in different paths.*
> (Kailasapathy 1987, 391)

And they challenged even widely accepted notions such as
rebirth:

> *Milk does not return to the udder,*
> *Likewise butter can never become butter-milk;*
> *The sound of the conch does not exist once it is broken;*
> *The blown flower, the fallen fruit do not go back to the tree;*
> *The dead are never born again, never.*
> (Ibid., 401)

Around the twelfth–thirteenth centuries, the Varkari movement
in Maharashtra also began. It centred around pilgrimages in which
thousands, and later hundreds of thousands, of people walked (made
the *vari*) to Pandharpur to view the deity Vitthala. As a relatively
more documented movement, with hundreds of *sant*s (holy men),
an analysis here gives us a full description of the radical bhakti

movement, as opposed to conservatives like Ramdas in Maharashtra and Vallabhacharya in north India.

The main difference perhaps was that the sants of the medieval and early modern period—twelfth to seventeenth centuries—were householders, living off their labour, working as farmers, artisans, even common labourers. This was in contrast to the more orthodox, who had maths and other institutions behind them. Tukaram, the great seventeenth century Marathi sant, stressed this in one of his songs:

I've no followers to dispense
stories of my holiness.
I'm no lord of a hermitage,
no habit of holding on to land.
I don't keep a shop
for idol worshippers to stop.
(Tukaram 1973, #272)

This meant that they also had families: they were householder-saints, which was something new for the lower castes in Indian history. They lived with their wives and children, supporting them with their labour. Even with Buddhism, the main ideal was renunciation; it was the *bhikkus* of the Sangha who were the role models for the society. Now, spirituality was brought into the world in a new way.

However, this was not to the liking of brahmanism. The hagiographers who later wrote the 'lives' of the sants—especially Priyadas, in eighteenth century north India, and Mahipati in eighteenth century Maharashtra—invariably depicted them as ineffective artisans and merchants, and their wives as shrews. Sants, especially shudra sants, were not supposed to be householders. The brahman hagiographers also refused to admit the 'dalit' and 'Muslim' identity of sants like Kabir, arguing in the case of Kabir that he was born of a brahman family but adopted by Muslims, and in the case of Ravidas that he had been a brahman in a previous birth born into an untouchable family for the 'sin' of accidentally feeding meat to his guru; according to Priyadas, he even refused to drink his mother's milk until commanded to be God!

before colo [handwritten note]

The Varkari movement arose in the twelfth century, led by the tailor Namdev and the outcaste brahman Dnandev. There was undoubtedly some influence from the Lingayat movement. In fact, Basava had himself served for decades in Mangavedha, now a town in Maharashtra that was part of the Kalyana kingdom at the time; it is the home of the untouchable sant of that period, Cokhamela. But there is no historical record of this influence. Though Vitthala himself (herself? The deity is frequently spoken of as feminine—Vitthai or Vitthu Mawali, and the image too, looks quite feminine) is of Kannada origin, this connection is lost. The Varkaris identified as 'Vishnudas' (not as 'Hindu'!), and perhaps the 'Saivite' identification of the Lingayats was an obstacle to admitting a connection.

As a brahman, Dnandev is given the credit of being 'founder' and theorist, but it was Nama who wandered through north India, Nama whose writings are collected in the Guru Granth Sahib of the Sikhs, Nama who is known to the later north Indian sants such as Kabir and Ravidas and to Nanak, the founder of Sikhism. The links thus run from Maharashtra to north and west India, while the southern bhakti movements remained separate.

On the thematic plane, the defining features of the radical bhakti movements were their rejection of caste and priestly ritualism. As one song attributed to Nama put it,

> No need of doing vows, austerities, or pilgrimages—
> Be content with hymns to Hari at home.
> You don't have to exclude anything of life or food,
> Place your every mood at Hari's feet,
> You don't have to sacrifice, meditate or give up sex;
> Your devotion will suffice, laid at Hari's feet.
> Nama says, hold the name firmly on your tongue,
> It will give you a meeting with Pandurang.
> (Namdev 1999, #1371)

The theme was "*na lage*"—you don't have to do this or that. The radical sants and their followers expressed their devotion in singing and dancing, and if there were no open intermarriages, at least they insisted on dining together and rejection of hierarchy.

In North India the tradition was exemplified most thoroughly with Kabir and Ravidas. Kabir, though born in a (Muslim) family, attacked *mullahs* as well as *pundits*, was against ritualism and questioned caste.

Worship, libations, six sacred rites,
this dharma's full of ritual blights.
Four ages teaching Gayatri, I ask you, who won liberty?
You wash your body if you touch another,
tell me who could be lower than you?
Proud of your merit, puffed up with your rights,
no good comes out of such great pride
How could he whose very name
is pride-destroyer endure the same?
Drop the limits of caste and clan,
seek for freedom's space,
destroy the shoot, destroy the seed,
seek the unembodied place.
(Kabir 1997, 35; translation mine)

Kabir could put things very fiercely. Ravidas' general poetry was not so fierce, but it has given us one of the most beautiful expressions of a vision of utopia from a very early period. The poem is 'Begumpura' (The City without Sorrow):

The regal realm with the sorrowless name,
they call it Begumpura, a place with no pain,
No taxes or cares, nor own property there,
no wrongdoing, worry, terror or torture.
Oh my brother, I've come to take it as my own,
my distant home, where everything is right.
That imperial kingdom is rich and secure,
where none are third or second—all are one;
Its food and drink are famous, and those who live there
dwell in satisfaction and in wealth.
They do this or that, they walk where they wish,
they stroll through fabled palaces unchallenged.
Oh, says Ravidas, a tanner now set free,
those who walk beside me are my friends.
(Hawley and Juergensmeier 1988, 32)

The bhakti version of 'dalit visions' did not give an analysis of the aspects of brahmanic Hinduism which it rejected; how and why caste and priestly ritualism arose and what their function was in society was not its concern. Its expression was in a vision of ecstasy of another possible world. By the eighteenth century also this was recuperated by a resurgent brahmanism, finding a base in the newly arising independent and regionally based kingdoms. The Peshwa in Maharashtra was highly orthodox; Ranjit Singh's Sikh empire gave a base of power to aspiring Jat peasants, but left untouchability alive within Sikhism itself.

Four

Hinduism as Brahman Exploitation
Jotiba Phule

The extreme fertility of the soil of India, its rich productions, the proverbial wealth of the people, and the other innumerable gifts which this favourable land enjoys, and which have more recently tempted the cupidity of the Western Nations, attracted the Aryans.... The original inhabitants with whom these earth-born gods, the Brahmans, fought, were not inappropriately termed Rakshasas, that is the protectors of the land. The incredible and foolish legends regarding their form and shape are no doubt mere chimeras, the fact being that these people were of superior stature and hardy make.... The cruelties which the European settlers practised on the American Indians on their first settlement in the new world had certainly their parallel in India in the advent of the Aryans and their subjugation of the aborigines.... This, in short, is the history of Brahman domination in India. They originally settled on the banks of the Ganges whence they spread gradually over the whole of India. In order, however, to keep a better hold on the people they devised that weird system of mythology, the ordination of caste, and the code of crude and inhuman laws to which we can find no parallel among the other nations. (Phule 1990, 118–20)

Phule's *Gulamgiri*, written in Marathi but with an English introduction, was published in 1885, the year of the founding of the Indian National Congress, but before the full-scale upsurge of Hindu nationalism and also before the principal proponent of radical nationalism, Bal Gangadhar Tilak, had become identified with social orthodoxy. The brahmans whom Phule attacked so strongly were not only the orthodox. They also included the 'moderates', liberals and reformers, grouped in organisations such as the Prarthana Samaj, Brahma Samaj, Sarvajanik Sabha and the Congress. All of these were seen by him as elite efforts, designed to deceive the masses and establish upper-caste hegemony. Caste, to him, was *slavery*, as vicious and brutal as the enslavement of the Africans in the United States, but based in India not only on open conquest and subordination but also on deception and religious illusion. This deception was the essence of what the high castes called 'Hinduism'.

Jotiba Phule (1826–1890) was not a dalit himself, but a man of what would today be described as an 'affluent OBC' caste, the Malis, gardeners by traditional occupation and classed with the Maratha-Kunbis as people of middle status. While he developed a strong dalit following, his main organisational work was in fact among the middle-to-low non-brahman castes of Maharashtra, traditionally classed as shudras and known till today as the *bahujan samaj*. He began as a social reformer establishing schools for both girls and untouchable boys, and founded the Satyashodhak Samaj in 1875, which organised the non-brahmans to propound rationality, the giving up of brahman priests for rituals and the education of children (both boys and girls). His major writings include plays, poems and polemical works—poems attacking brahmanism, a ballad on Shivaji, and three books: *Gulamgiri* which mainly focuses on caste; *Shetkaryaca Asud*, describing the oppression of the peasants; and *Sarvajanik Satya Dharm*, an effort to outline anew, theistic and egalitarian religion.

At the theoretical level too, Phule sought to unite the shudras (non-brahmans) and ati-shudras (dalits). He argued that the latter were not only more oppressed but had been downgraded because of their earlier heroism in fighting brahman domination. More importantly, he argued that shudras and ati-shudras together represented an oppressed and exploited mass, and compared their subordination with that of the native Indians in the Americas and the Blacks. Phule's broadsides are, in fact, an expression of a theory not simply of religious domination and conquest, but of exploitation.

The Aryan race theory, the dominant explanation of caste and Indian society in his time, provided the framework for his theory. This had been made the centre of discourse by the European 'Orientalists' who saw the Vedas as an ancient spiritual link between Europeans and Indians, by the British administrators and census takers who classified the society they ruled, and by the Indian elite—people like Tilak—who used it to justify brahman superiority. Phule turned it on its head, in a way somewhat akin to Marx turning Hegelian dialectics on its head, to formulate a theory of contradiction and exploitation: brahmans were indeed descended from conquering Indo-Europeans, but far from being superior, they were cruel and violent invaders who had overturned an originally prosperous and egalitarian society, using every kind of deceit and violence to do so, forging a mythology which was worse than all others since it was in principle based on inequality and forbade the conquered masses from even studying its texts.

By inverting the traditional Aryan theory, Phule took his critique of brahmanism and caste to a mass level. He used it to radically reinterpret puranic mythology, seeing the various *avatars* of Vishnu as stages in the conquest of India, while taking the *rakshasas* as heroes of the people. Central to this interpretation was the figure of Bali Raja. In Phule's re-figuration of the myth, Bali Raja was the original king of Maharashtra, reigning over an ideal state of beneficence, castelessness and prosperity, with the popular gods of the regions (Khandoba, Jotiba, Naikba, etc.) depicted as his officials. The puranic myth in which the brahman boy Waman asks three boons of Bali and then steps on his chest to send him down to hell is taken by Phule as a story of deception and conquest by the invading Aryans. This reinterpretation had a strong resonance with popular culture, for in Maharashtra (as in other parts of south India, particularly Kerala) Bali is indeed seen as a popular and 'peasant' king, and is remembered with the Marathi saying, "*ida pida javo, Balica rajya yevo*" (let troubles and sorrows go and the kingdom of Bali come). Similarly, the popular religious festivals of the rural areas are fairs centring around non-Vedic gods, all of whom (except the most widely known, Vithoba) continue to have non-brahman priests. Phule's alternative mythology woven around Bali Raja, could evoke an image of a peasant community, and his anti-Vedic, anti-Aryan and anti-caste equalitarian message with its use of poetry, dialogue, and drama, could reach beyond the literate elite to a wider audience of non-brahmans.

Phule's was not simply a focus on ideology and culture; he stressed equally the factors of violence and conquest in history (those which Marx had relegated to the realm of "primitive accumulation of capital") and took the peasant community as his centre. Violence and force were overriding realities in all historical processes; the 'Aryan conquest' was simply the first of a series of invasions and conquests of the subcontinent, the Muslim and the British being the other major ones. It was, if anything, worse than the others not for racial reasons but for the fact that the 'Irani Aryabhats' solidified their power using a hierarchical and inequalitarian religious ideology. Brahman rule, or *bhatshahi*, was a regime that used state power and religious hegemony to maintain exploitation. The key exploited class/group was the peasantry, the key exploiters the bureaucracy which the brahmans dominated even under colonial rule. Taxes, cesses and state takeover of peasant lands were the crucial mechanisms of extracting surplus, supplemented by moneylending and extortion for religious programmes. Phule's ethnographic descriptions of peasant poverty, his sensitivity to issues of drought and land use and to what would today be called watershed development, and his condemnation of the forest bureaucracy make him strikingly modern in many ways.

Phule's theory can be looked at as a kind of incipient historical materialism in which economic exploitation and cultural dominance are interwoven. In contrast to a class theory, communities become the basis for contradiction (the shudra-ati-shudra peasantry versus the brahman bureaucracy and religious order); in contrast to changing property relations, conquest, force, state power and ideology are seen as driving factors.

Phule is today taken as a founding figure in Maharashtra not simply by the anti-caste but also by the farmers', women's and rural-based environmental movements. Apropos women, his personal life stands in contrast to the compromises made by almost every other social reformer and radical: he not only educated his wife, Savitribai and encouraged her to become a teacher in a school for girls, but also resolutely withstood all community pressures to take a second wife in spite of their childlessness. His writings assimilated women into his general theories of conquest and violence (seeing them as the primary victims of force and violence, emphasising the miserable life of peasant women). However, in his later years and under the influence of the great feminist radicals of his day such as Pandita Ramabai and Tarabai Shinde, he took a stronger position describing male patriarchal power as a specific form of exploitation. The 'double standard' which oppressed women was prevalent, he argued, not only as seen in the pitiable conditions of brahman widows, but also in the patriarchy of shudra households in which the woman was expected to remain a loyal *pativrata* (a woman who is loyal to her husband) while the man was free to have as many women as he wanted.

Like all major dalits and spokesmen for the low-castes, Phule felt the need to establish a religious alternative, and his last major book, *Sarvajanik Satya Dharma*, details a noble-minded equalitarian theism, which also projects a strong male-female equality. In contrast to a secularism which assumes a Hindu majority and ignores all the problems associated with it, Phule attacked Hinduism at every point, challenging its legitimacy and questioning its existence. What is striking in his works is his refusal to even recognise 'Hinduism' as such: to him it is not a legitimate religion but superstition, a bag of tricks, a weapon of domination. Thus he can refer in *Sarvajanik Satya Dharma* to the ideal family in which the father becomes a Buddhist, the mother a Christian, the daughter a Muslim, and the son a Satyadharmist—where there is no scope for a 'Hindu' (see *Collected Works* 1991, 39–40). He never treats brahmans as simply a racial category, a group which is unalterably evil; but to be accepted they would have to give up their claim to a religion which makes them 'earth-gods':

> When all the Aryabhat Brahmans throw away their bogus scriptures and begin to behave towards all human beings in the way of Truth, then there is no doubt that all women and men will bow down

reverently before the Creator of all and pray for the welfare of the Aryas. (Ibid., 32)

An appreciation of Phule's thought is only at the beginning stage in most of India. OBCs (ex-shudras) have been slow to organise, and it is only in the last couple of decades that he is becoming more widely known. He wrote almost entirely in Marathi and in his time was little known outside Maharashtra. For a long time the lack of a communication network among low castes and the revulsion for his writings felt by most of the brahman elite made his work inaccessible. Even dalits often ignored him ("the problem with Phule is that he has no caste behind him," as one non-brahman radical activist commented) and although Ambedkar acknowledged him as one of his 'gurus', very little of Phules's influence is actually seen in Ambedkar's writings. The Phule-Ambedkar centenary year (November 1990 marked Phule's death centenary and April 1991 Ambedkar's birth centenary), however, saw an upsurge of interest throughout India. Kanshiram's BSP did much to popularise Phule along with Periyar and Shahu Maharaj in northern India. Recently, the feminist scholar Uma Chakravarti has described Phule as a forerunner elaborating the theory of "brahmanical patriarchy" (see Chakravarti 1998; 1983; 1993; 1981), while in a centenary year seminar organised by the Centre for Social Studies at Surat, G. P. Deshpande argued "that Phule was the first Indian system builder" providing a "logic of history", as Hegel did in Europe:

> Phule's thought proved that socio-political struggles of the Indian people could generate universal criterion. Phule also talked about knowledge and power much before Foucault did. In fact, Foucault's postmodernist analysis comes at a time when Europe has literally seen the 'end of history' whereas Phule's efforts were to change the world/society with the weapon of knowledge. (Phule 1991, ix–x)

Phule's argument that knowledge, education and science were weapons of advance for the exploited masses, was in contrast to all elitist theories that sought to link western science and eastern morals and argue that Indians could maintain their (brahmanical) traditions while adopting science and technology from the west for material development. For Phule, rather, *vidya* or knowledge was in direct contrast with the brahmanic, ritualistic *shastra* and was a weapon for equality and human freedom as well as economic advance. He constantly stressed the need for shudras and ati-shudras to stand forth and think on their own, and his response to the ideological confusions of his day sounds strikingly 'postmodern':

All ideologies have decayed,
no one views comprehensively.
What is trivial, what is great
cannot be understood.
Philosophies fill the market,
gods have become a cacophony;
to the enticements of desire
people fall prey.
All, everywhere it has decayed;
truth and untruth cannot be assayed;
this is how, people have become one
everywhere.
There is a cacophony of opinions,
no one heeds another;
each one thinks the opinion
he has found is great.
Pride in untruth
dooms them to destruction—
so the wise people say,
seek truth.
(Phule 1990, 440; translated by Gail Omvedt and Bharat Patankar)

Five

Hinduism as Patriarchy

Ramabai, Tarabai and the early Feminists

Due to the efforts of Pandita Ramabai there was a beginning of education for girls and many great learned Arya Brahmans began to educate their helpless ignorant women to redress the errors of their rishi ancestors, but there may be many negative results of our critical writing about the tyrannical statements of the merciless Aryan bookwriters on women. Mainly this: fearing that when the cruel wickedness of the Aryan books come to the attention of the daughters of bhat-brahmans they will make mincemeat of all the legends of the temples and gods and mockingly reject them, and that besides, in most Brahman families a continual quarrel between mothers-in-law and daughters-in-law will arise and cause numerous tensions, many bhat-bhikshuks will stop sending their daughters and daughters-in-law to school and naturally will not give them even so much a glimpse of our *Satsar* book. (Phule 1990, 372)

Phule wrote this in a pamphlet in 1885 in response to attacks on two women, Tarabai Shinde and Pandita Ramabai. In 1882, Ramabai had come to Pune, founded the Arya Mahila Samaj and then, shortly after, departed for England where she converted to Christianity. For this, she was condemned by even the moderate brahmans who had originally sponsored her efforts. Tarabai, the daughter of one of Phule's Maratha colleagues in the Satyashodhak Samaj, had written a bitter and hard-hitting attack on Hindu patriarchy, *Stri-Purush Tulna* ('Comparison of Women and Men') in 1882. Both women evoked waves of reaction—Ramabai in the wider world of the English-educated brahman intellectuals, Tarabai in Phule's own Satyashodhak circles; and Phule defended both (on Ramabai, see Chakravarti 1998; Kosambi 1992).

Of course, Phule's 'feminist' leanings had expressed themselves earlier; in his educating his own wife and refusing to divorce her even though they had no children. Savitribai was the first, in many ways, of the nineteenth century Maharashtrian feminists, taking up with enthusiasm the teaching of dalit boys and girls in the schools that Phule had founded, enduring the abuse and dung-throwing of brahman women as she went to her work. After his death also, she carried on, dying finally of the plague which she had caught because of her nursing activity. She thus remains one of the earliest role models of happily married feminist women.

Neither Ramabai nor Tarabai, however, were happily married. Their story was of a more familiar feminist kind, having to fight patriarchy both in the society and in the family.

Pandita Ramabai was by far the better known of the two women and, in spite of her conversion to Christianity, accepted much of the framework of the brahman intellectuals of the time. She called her organisation (undoubtedly the first autonomous women's organisation in India) the *Arya Mahila Samaj* and focused her main English book on 'the high-caste Hindu woman'. She also continued to retain many brahmanic habits, in particular vegetarianism, as a symbol of her Indian identity—perhaps a necessary symbol for her in the face of often racist church pressure—and accepted the identification of 'India' with 'Hindu' and the Aryan model justification for caste hierarchy, arguing that the complete dependence and ignorance of women had been the cause of "the present degradation of the Hindu nation" (Ramabai 1887, 48).

> Without doubt, 'caste' originated in the economic division of labour. The talented and most intelligent portion of the Aryan Hindus became, as was natural, the governing body of the entire race. (Ibid., 3)

In spite of this and for all the frequent mildness of her language, it was Pandita Ramabai who was the first to proclaim, with great clarity, backed by her personal refusal to remain a Hindu, that the Sanskritic core of Hinduism was irrevocably and essentially anti-woman:

> Those who diligently and impartially read Sanskrit literature in the original, cannot fail to recognize the law-giver Manu as one of those hundreds who have done their best to make women hateful beings in the world's eye.... I can say honestly and truthfully, that I have never read any sacred book in Sanskrit literature without meeting this kind of hateful sentiment about women. (Ibid., 29)

Thus her conversion testimony stressed that there were

> ... only two things on which all those books, the Dharma Shastras, the sacred epics, the Puranas and the modern poets, the popular preachers of the present day and orthodox high-caste men, were agreed: that women of high and low caste as a class, were bad, very bad, worse than demons, as unholy as untruth, and that they could not get Moksha as men [could]. (Cited in Kosambi 1992, 63)

In other words, in spite of her initial acceptance of most of the assumptions of Hindu nationalism, when it came to her own experience, this daughter of a wandering and reformist brahman, the only woman of her time to have been educated in the sacred language, who had fought her way forward to be recognised by the intellectuals of her time, had come to condemn the core of Hinduism as fundamentally patriarchal. And, though she started with a focus on upper-caste widows, this changed when she confronted the plague of the late 1990s. She made a bold decision, went to the worst areas in Madhya Pradesh, and brought back hundreds of girls, helpless and starving. Here she began to abandon the caste-related prejudices, and when it became impossible to house the girls in her *Sharda Sadan* in Pune, she bought land in a nearby village, Kedgaon, setting up a feminist community, with women learning all kinds of artisanal, agricultural and industrial skills—a self-reliant utopia. Pandita Ramabai was thus one of the first to actually embody a vision of a casteless-classless and patriarchy-free society in a functioning community.

Harsher than Ramabai's writings were those of Tarabai Shinde. We know little of her life and virtually nothing of what happened to her after she wrote her book. It is clear that she did not go on to achieve the autonomy she so clearly strove for, and whether she ever managed to carve out even a small space for herself in the confined world of the nineteenth century Maratha landholding elite is something we shall perhaps never know. (Such spaces did exist, but were available to very few). *Stri-Purush Tulna* is her sole known testament, and the sound of a voice not-so-far-heard is its beginning:

> Since this is my first effort at writing, being helpless, bound and without a voice in the prison house of the endless Maratha customs, this essay has extremely harsh language. But seeing that the new terrible examples of men's arrogance and one-sided morality that appear every day are ignored and all blame is put on women, my mind has been filled with the pride of women's position and gone into utmost turmoil. (Shinde 1992; translation mine)

Tarabai was referring to the debate on widows who were blamed for trying to dispose their babies, the implications of sexual assaults on them being ignored. She was concerned about more than just atrocities; she attacked the whole pattern of life laid out for women.

> What is *stri dharma?* Endless devotion to a single husband, behaving according to his whims. Even if he beats her, curses her, keeps a prostitute, drinks, robs the treasury, takes bribes, when he returns home she should worship him as a god, as if Krishna Maharaj himself had come from stealing the milk of the Gavalis ... There are a million reasons for breaking *pativrata*.

And she went on from this to a scornful, satirical attack on the gods and rishis of the puranas themselves:

> Now, even with five husbands didn't Draupadi have to worry about Kama Maharaj's intentions?... [What about Satyavati and Kunti?] One agreed to the whims of a rishi in order to remove the bad odour from her body, the other obeyed a mantra! What wonderful gods! What wonderful rishis! (Ibid., 6)

Stri-Purush Tulna takes the form of a diffuse and bitter polemic. It is not a reasoned, direct critique of the Hindu scriptures based on conceptual analysis, but a satirical attack on them in a language of familiarity. This was in fact the way in which many working class and peasant women talked about the stories they were so familiar with. The Ramayana and the Mahabharata were a part of the lives of the majority but this did not necessarily make them part of a religion, as was made out by spokesmen of the emerging Hinduism. When Brahmanic theorists began to turn such texts into 'scriptures', women like Tarabai and Ramabai had to attack and reject them. Ramabai tried to create a different institutional framework with different human relations, and spent a lifetime in the service of high (and low) caste widows, whose position represented the most dire fate of women at the time. Tarabai, who was not in a position to do as much, expressed her rebellion in a bitter rhetorical attack on the structures of patriarchy:

> It was a woman, Savitri, who went to the court of Yama in order to save the life of her husband. But leave aside Yama's court, have you heard of any men who have gone even a step on the path towards it? Just as a woman loses her auspiciousness and so has to bury her face like a convict and live all her life in darkness, do you have to shave your beard and live like a hermit the rest of your life if your wife dies? If any smart alec god gave you a certificate to take another woman on the tenth day after your wife has died, then show it to me! (Ibid., 8)

In their different ways, women like Tarabai and Ramabai were already, in the nineteenth century, raising their voices against what Partha Chatterjee has described as the "nationalist resolution of the women's question." This rested on separating the material and cultural spheres and making women the guardians of the home, its moral and spiritual essence:

> What was necessary was to cultivate the material techniques of modern western civilization while retaining and strengthening the distinctive spiritual essence of the national culture. (Chatterjee 1989, 238)

In looking to this solution of 'eastern morals and western science', there seems to have been no qualitative distinction between reformist Hindus and Hindu nationalists. This was insufficient for women who wanted to be considered complete human beings, since it was the 'eastern morals' which oppressed them. (Whether 'western morals' also did so is another issue; in fact Ramabai, to take the most obvious example, found herself in many conflicts with her Christian guides regarding attitudes towards women after her conversion.)

Unlike the Arya Samajists, for instance, Ramabai could not see the present state of women simply as 'degeneration'. Unlike the Brahmo Samajists and men like Gandhi, she could not turn to idealised versions of the Vedas and Upanishads to convince herself that the 'essence' of Hindu spiritualism could be saved from its casteist and patriarchal excrescences. Ramabai, like Phule and the later militant dalits, had to reject Hinduism. Similarly, Tarabai could not see rishis and gods as symbols of divinity without accepting her own position as an inferior. Yet how is it that so many of the later and more highly placed women activists came to compromise on these issues? The answer is partly, of course, that they were forced to: compromise was a way to make some small gains.

After the upsurge of Hindu nationalism in the late nineteenth century had forced even the moderate social reformism of the upper castes to retreat, the women's movement slowly took on an organised form. It emerged with some autonomy in the 1920s with the founding of the All-India Women's Congress and similar organisations. These upper-caste and elite women's organisations worked within the Hindu framework and spoke of Sita and Savitri as ideals for women, not as symbols of male oppression. They praised the freedom of the Vedic period, and depicted *purdah* and other evils as resulting from the social conditions of the Muslim invasion, if not from the Muslims themselves. They fought for (and eventually got implemented in some form) a new Hindu code giving substantial, though hardly equal, rights to women in such sensitive areas as property and divorce. But they were embarrassed by the fact that a dalit, Ambedkar, was the chairman of its drafting committee; and they had no organisation to combat the street demonstrations organised by the fundamentalists. Further, by leaving Muslim women out of the bill, they left a dangerous legacy for the fomentation of communal feelings in later years (see Everett 1981).

Peasant women seem to have had their own forms of action that reinterpreted tradition more actively but very often also remained within the framework of the Hindu discourse while building an organisational space for women. Kapil Kumar describes the role of women led by Jaggi (a Kurmi) in the Oudh Kisan Sabha, supported by Baba Ramchandra (a Maharashtrian brahman). This led to the founding of a women's front, the Kisanin Sabha, which focused both on giving women land rights, and attacking male polygamy and reforming family relations. Like Phule, the Kisanin Sabha argued for monogamy. Its rules stated that all relationships should be treated as legitimate and that women should be respected even if they did not produce children (Kumar 1989, 351). In addition, while using local religious traditions (like celebrating a success with a *yagya* to a village goddess), there was also a reinterpretation of tradition. Thus Kaikeyi was praised for sending Rama to the jungle, and Sita was viewed as a woman who acted on her own: "Did not Rama tell Sita not to accompany him to the forest but Sita on her own decided to go?" (Ibid., 363; quote from an interview with Jaggi)

There is very little historical evidence, and even less effort to uncover what may exist, of the actual discourse and actions of working class and peasant women throughout this period while their elite sisters were yielding to the male formulations of Hindu nationalist themes, whether those of Hindu *raj* or Ram raj. Sumanta Banerjee offers a clue to what could be done in his depiction of lower class women's culture in nineteenth-century Calcutta. He writes of the *kheur*, a popular form of songs on the Radha-Krishna theme, which evolved into a kind of drama of repartee. He cites one example in which Ambalika protests when her mother Satyavati urges her to have union with Vyasa to beget a child:

> People say
> as a girl you used to row a boat in the river.
> Seeing your beauty, tempted by your lotus-bud,
> the great Parashar stung you, and
> there was a hue and cry:

You've done it once,
You don't have anything to fear.
Now you can do as much as you want to,
no one will say anything.
If it has to be done,
Why don't you do it, mother?
(Banerjee 1981, 138–39)

Such forms of expression were used by many lower class women. Similar biting dialogues were apparently also used in the Satyashodhak *tamasha*s of the 1920s in Maharashtra and seem to have been common to tamasha culture in most parts of India. The logical style of the Ambalika song (if you think it's so great, do it yourself) was a theme natural to lower caste men and women. It was used in a very different context a century later at the time of the founding of the Dalit Panthers and provoked an uproar in the intellectual circles of Bombay. The occasion was a reading of Namdev Dhasal's poetry *Golpitha*, focused on the 'redlight' district of Mumbai. Speaking at the time, a prominent Marathi writer said that, "prostitutes do work necessary to society and so should be given respect", and the reply was given by one of the Panther poets, Raja Dhale, who said, "If Durgabai thinks the work deserves so much respect, why doesn't she do it herself?"

The powerful critiques of the early feminists, women like Ramabai and Tarabai and their male supporters, focused on crucial issues of patriarchy and sexuality, attacking the double standard of pativrata. Many women upheld the value of monogamy and others used legends and mythology to mock all impositions of sexual standards, though no explicit claims to sexual freedom were raised among reformers and radicals. Later, leaders of the women's movement during the colonial period, identified with the dominant Hindu reformist cultural trend underlying the Congress organisations and in so doing, accepted the basic framework of brahmanical patriarchy. But it was early feminists like Ramabai and Tarabai who were closer to the general attitude of lower class and peasant women in taking the puranas as stories and not scriptures, and seeing them as representing the many facets of male oppression rather than as divinely-ordained ideals of human relationships.

What of Phule's confidence, though, that education would lead even brahman women to throw away the shastras? For some it has undoubtedly happened. Yet education has not proved to be the great dissolver of patriarchy that it was expected to be, perhaps because education in independent India has been limited, focused on rote memory only, and fashioned within the framework of the successfully constructed brahmanic Hinduism.

Six

Hinduism as Aryan Conquest

The Dalit Radicals of the 1920s

The mobilisation of the oppressed and exploited sections of society—
the peasants, dalits, women and low castes that Phule had spoken of
as shudras and ati-shudras—occurred on a large scale in the 1920s
and 1930s, under varying leaderships and with varying ideologies.
They took part in nationalist campaigns, some of them hailing
Gandhi as a kind of messianic figure; they organised unions and
kisan sabhas; they staged strikes, anti-rent campaigns and revenue/
tax boycotts; they fought for forest and village commons. It was
an era, following the first World War and the Russian Revolution,
when the masses were coming on to the stage of history.

Inevitably, the specificities of caste exploitation could not be
ignored in India. Many low-caste activists of the 1920s, organising
as non-brahmans and dalits, were drawn to an anti-caste, anti-
brahman, even anti-Hindu ideology of the kind that Phule had
formulated. Since few outside Maharashtra had heard of Phule,
most likely it was the Tamil non-brahman movement which had
the most influence as the strongest initiator of 'non-Aryan' themes.
Yet so pervasive were these that it is clear the themes struck a deep
mass resonance everywhere. The very use of 'Aryan' discourse by
the elite was evoking a common response which, in its turn, was
to force the elite to revise this discourse significantly. The non-
brahman movements in Maharashtra and Tamil Nadu, as well as

the dalit movements arising in places as distant as the Punjab and Karnataka, all began to argue in terms of the Aryan conquest and brahman exploitation through religion.

The new identities that most of the dalits adopted in the 1920s—Ad-Dharm in Punjab, Adi-Hindu in UP and Hyderabad, Adi-Dravida, Adi-Andhra and Adi-Karnataka in south India—indicated a common claim to being original inhabitants. This was exemplified early in Maharashtra, where a pre-Ambedkar dalit leader, Kisan Faguji Bansode (1870–1946), warned his caste Hindu friends in 1909 that:

> The Aryans—your ancestors—conquered us and gave us unbearable harassment. At that time we were your conquest, you treated us even worse than slaves and subjected us to any torture you wanted. But now we are no longer your subjects, we have no service relationship with you, we are not your slaves or serfs....We have had enough of the harassment and torture of the Hindus. (Bhagwat 1980, 297)

Bansode, an educator and journalist, represented a generation of educated Mahar leaders that arose in Nagpur, where Mahars often had some land and formed forty per cent of the workers in an emerging textile industry. He, like many other of the regional Mahar leadership, later turned away from such themes, identifying with Hinduism through devotion to the Mahar saint Chokamela, and Ambedkar in fact had to fight this group to establish, his own leadership in Vidarbha (see Omvedt 1994, chapter 3). However, by the 1920s, the new dalit or 'adi' movements, with an ideological claim to being heirs of a 'non-Aryan' or 'original Indian' equalitarian tradition, began to take off in many regions of India.

In Andhra, where the process was affected by the militant Dravidianism of the Madras presidency, the commercialised coastal areas produced both a mobile dalit agricultural labourer class and a small educated section. A proposed conference of dalits in Vijayawada in 1917, sponsored by reformist Hindus, was to be called the First Provincial Panchama Mahajana Sabha but changed its name, in a mood of revolt, to the Adi-Andhra Mahajana Sabha on the grounds that "the so-called Panchamas were the original sons of the soil and they were the rulers of the country" (cited in Gautam 1976, 67). The dalits were in a militant mood; the major temple in the city closed down for the three days of their conference. For over a decade and a half after that, until they became absorbed as 'harijans' into the Congress and Communist movements, coastal Andhra dalits held conferences as Adi-Andhras. By the 1931 census, nearly a third of the Malas and Madigas of the Madras presidency had given their identity as Adi-Andhra.

The Vijayawada conference was presided over by Bhagyareddy Varma (1888–1939), a Hyderabad dalit originally named Madari Bhagaiah, who had been organising Adi-Hindu conferences since 1912. Hyderabad had a vigorous, though factionalised, petty bourgeois dalit group, which began to pick up the Adi-Hindu identity in the 1920s. By 1930 the state census indicated a rather vigorous cultural debate:

> The Adi-Dravida Educational League argued that, judged by the history, philosophy and civilization of the Adi-Dravidas, the real aborigines of the Deccan, the depressed classes are, as a community, entirely separate and distinct from the followers of Vedic religion, called Hindus. The League's contention was that Hinduism is not the ancestral religion of the aborigines of Hindustan; that the non-Vedic communities of India object to being called Hindu because of their inherited abhorrence of the doctrines of the Manusmruti and like scriptures, who have distinguished themselves from caste Hindus for centuries past, that the Vedic religion which the Aryans brought in the wake of their invasion was actively practiced upon the non-Vedic aborigines, and that the aborigines, coming under the influence of the Hindus, gradually and half-consciously adopted Hindu ideas and prejudices. (*Census of India* 1933, 258)

In Hyderabad, thus, Tamil dalits identified themselves as Adi-Dravidas. Telugu-speaking dalits called themselves Adi-Hindus but a large section of them gave this a militant, anti-brahman interpretation. Bhagyareddy Varma was a major figure in this group, later identifying with Buddhism and giving tacit support to a younger generation of radicals who became followers of Ambedkar. In faraway UP too; where Varma travelled for conferences, a new radical identity arose. Its leading ideologue was an untouchable ascetic from Mainpuri district who had briefly been a member of the Arya Samaj. He left it out of disgust and began to organise the dalits on the basis of an Adi-Hindu identity. Calling himself, rather defiantly, Acchutananda, he argued:

> The untouchables, the so-called harijans, are in fact adi-Hindu, i.e., the original or autochthonous Nagas or Dasas of the north and the Dravidas of the south of the subcontinent, and they are the undisputed, heavenly owners of Bharat. All others are immigrants to the land, including the Aryans, who conquered the original populations not by valour but by deceit and manipulation ... by usurping others' rights, subjugating the peace-loving and rendering the self-sufficient people indigents and slaves. Those who ardently believed in equality were ranked, and ranked lowest. The Hindus and untouchables have since always remained poles apart. (Quoted in Khare 1984, 85; see also Lynch 1969)

In Punjab, a dalit named Mangoo Ram, also originally a part of the Arya Samaj, began an Ad-Dharm movement in which the dalits by 1926, had proclaimed themselves a separate *quaum* (community) in a conference in a village of Hoshiarpur district. As the report of the Ad-Dharm Mandal described the Aryan conquest:

> During this time of great achievements, the Aryans heard about the original land's civilization and came there. They learned the art of fighting from the local inhabitants, and then turned against them. There were many wars—six hundred years of fighting—and then the Aryans finally defeated our ancestors, the local inhabitants. Our forefathers ... were pushed back into the jungles and the mountains.... from that time to this time the Hindu Aryans have suppressed the original people. (Jeurgensmeier 1982, 296)

Again there was a concern for official record of identity. By the 1931 census, nearly 500,000 Ad-Dharmis were reported.

Mangoo Ram, Acchutananda, Bhagyareddy Varma and Kisan Bansode were all of a generation slightly older than Ambedkar. They represented a new movement. They were able to build movements because untouchables, even in the villages, had gained some mobility, some access to education. Some went into the new factories and industries that were springing up as part of the limited industrialisation going on under British rule. Some were going overseas to plantations in Sri Lanka, Burma, Malaysia or as far as the west Indies; some went as soldiers in the Indian army, gaining both new status and physical as well as social mobility. All of this encouraged a new consciousness and awareness of rights. Others built a limited prosperity on the small holdings of land deriving from traditional village service-claims or even acquired from factory or other earnings. Spearheading the dalit organisations was a growing, though still small, educated or semi-educated leadership.

Various activities were taken up in this period. On the one hand, social reform included efforts to abolish *devadasi* traditions and sub-caste differences, to encourage cleanliness and the wearing of clothes indicating a solid social status and not village low-caste poverty. Many social reformers fought for giving up drinking or meat-eating; some were part of traditional *bhajan* groups in the radical bhakti tradition. But organising also occurred on economic issues; these involved fighting as factory and mill workers and new efforts to acquire land. Often a share of 'common' land was demanded from the Government.

While much of this involved linkages with reformist Hindus and acceptance of a basic Hinduist discourse, it was the 'adi' ideologies, based on non-Aryan racial theories, that provided the framework for the most militant expressions. It was not that all dalits, let alone all militant non-brahmans, accepted this; there were in every region those who chose instead to identify themselves as Hindus, fighting for temple entry, for instance. One set of dalit leaders, including some rivals of Ambedkar, even went over to the Hindu Mahasabha (this was fuelled by the ability of the brahman ideological leadership to define the bhakti movement as 'Hindu'). But the adi ideologies were pervasive ideas that won a popular base, as census reports show, and expressed the powerful emotional resistance to brahmanism and caste hierarchy that was embodied in dalit organisations everywhere in the colonial period. These also provided ideological links with the themes of the non-brahman movements of the Madras and Bombay presidencies, and most of the militant dalits also had some kind of alliance policy with the non-brahmans.

However, while these expressions bore similarities to the ideology of Phule, there were crucial differences from Phule's period that were reflected in the 1920s' non-brahman-dalit versions of the non-Aryan themes. First, a whole period of the construction of Hinduism had intervened, with the formulation of an increasingly sophisticated ideology of Hindu nationalism and its spread. The founding of major organisations such as the Hindu Mahasabha and the RSS occurred in this period. While the RSS remained an aloof, indrawn cadre organisation, organisations like the Mahasabha and the Arya Samaj undertook campaigns to win over low castes. The *shuddhi* campaign (designed to 'purify' dalits or convert them back from Islam) was centred primarily in the Punjab and north India, but the ideological appeals that went along with this had a much wider spread.

These identified dalits as part of the 'Hindu fold', and began to emphasise the low-caste origin of figures such as Valmiki and Vyasa to show that dalits too had a part in the 'creation of its great literature'. Thus for example the Chuhras, the other major north Indian caste were traditional rivals to the Chamars, and which provided the Bhangis or sweepers and latrine cleaners, were renamed as 'Balmikis' or 'Valmikis', given in effect a new identity. Along with this, the Hindu nationalist upper castes were revising and reinterpreting the racial aspect of their identity to stress a Hindu unity encompassing the caste hierarchy. By the 1930s, it was clear that this reinterpretation had an appeal: not only were large sections of non-brahmans identifying themselves as Hindus and claiming kshatriya status through the medium of caste conferences, but many important dalit leaders were also won over, with some like M. S. Rajah of Tamil Nadu and G. A. Gavai of Nagpur, joining the Hindu Mahasabha. This had to do with rivalries for leadership within the movement, but clearly the success of brahmanic Hinduism lay in creating scope to make use of such rivalries.

On the other hand, the dalit activists, peasants and workers of the time confronted the formulation of a radical class ideology by a new left intelligentsia. Young Indian socialists and communists led militant struggles that attracted large sections of the exploited and gave them a vision of an equalitarian society, but they avoided the recognition of caste and stressed a mechanical class framework that sought to override traditional identities rather than reinterpret them. It is striking that in the painful confrontation between Gandhi and Ambedkar after the Second Round Table Conference, when both Gandhians and Hindu Mahasabhaites tried to mobilise forces against the followers of Ambedkar and promote their solution to the issue, there was no prominent leftist even concerned about caste. Nehru in his autobiography remarks again and again that he saw Gandhi's harijan campaign as diversionary. 'It led to the diversion of the people's attention from the objective of full independence to the mundane cause of the upliftment of harijans' (Namboodiripad 1986, 492).

There were many aspects of this resistance to dealing with caste. There was an inability to even recognise identities such as the Adi-Andhra; the communists universally adopted the Gandhian term 'harijan' without much concern for whether it would appeal to the people concerned. It was an identity that to them was subordinate to and defined by the identity of untouchables as workers or (usually landless) peasants. They also saw themselves, without much trouble, as Hindu (perhaps as 'Hindu atheists'). Communists strikingly failed to win their own families away from traditional brahmanic Hindu rituals and practices, however much they may have ignored these personally. At the same time, communist class ideology defined the industrially-employed working class as advanced, while peasants (so crucial to Phule) were seen as backward, either feudal or 'petty bourgeois'. State exploitation (such as the exploitation of the peasantry by means of taxes and land revenue) was ignored, while only private property owners (moneylenders, zamindars, etc.) were the appropriate objects of class, as opposed to 'national' struggle.

As G. P. Deshpande has argued, Phule was making an effort to formulate a kind of universalistic ideology. He did not identify the oppressed and exploited shudras and ati-shudras as a set of castes so much as a peasant community, nor was the community strictly identified in racial terms. Non-Aryan was, after all, a negative category. In the 1920s, in contrast, the communists were putting forward another universalistic ideology. This one did not recognise community/caste as a node of exploitation; it threw all non-class categories into the realm of the superstructure, relegated to secondary consequence since they were only cultural/ideological constructs. *The formation of a class ideology of this type created a caste ideology of a specific type in reaction,* one which set up caste in opposition to class as a cultural/social factor, a non-economic factor.

In this context, with the strong ideological winds of Hindu nationalism (even in the modified form of Gandhism) and class struggle blowing all around them, the alternative 'adi' identity theories put forward by dalit radicals became racial ones. This can be seen in the above quotations. The Aryans as a people with one religion (Hinduism) were seen as basically confronting (conquering and enslaving) the non-Aryans as a people with a different religion. Sometimes the conquering Aryan caste/community was seen in larger terms (as 'all-caste Hinduism'), sometimes in smaller terms (only as the 'upper-castes'), but, more often, it was increasingly seen as a racially and religiously solidified group, 'the Hindus'. Phule had refused to legitimise Hinduism even as the religion of the supposed upper castes, seeing it only as a tool of exploitation. The later radicals also condemned Hinduism but began to see it more and more as a reality.

The communists saw the national movement as basically the only valid non-class struggle of the period, progressive because imperialism had to be fought in order to achieve a democratic revolution that would advance the development of the productive forces (i.e., industrialisation). This resulted in the dalit and non-brahman movements being stigmatised as pro-British, the communists refusing to recognise the legitimacy of taking the fight against the Indian elite (or 'Indian feudalism') as central.

Thus, two opposing ideologies prevailed among the toiling masses—one arguing from the standpoint of being original inhabitants or non-Aryans, and the other basing itself on the theory of class struggle. With the failure, in particular, of the more all-encompassing Marxist theory to incorporate the problems of caste in India, the broad movement of the oppressed was split into a class movement and a caste movement. There was no synthesis, no development of an integrated ideology and, as a result, those lower castes/classes who did get drawn into the national struggle or the left-led working class movement, gave up the sharpness of their anti-caste fight. Beneath the folds of the Congress and its hegemonic claim over almost all other political movements, a large number of forces and identities simmered but remained unconnected and ineffective.

The most significant attempt to transcend this fragmentation in the 1930s and 1940s was made by Dr B. R. Ambedkar, one of the great democratic leaders of the twentieth century.

Seven

Hinduism as Counter-Revolution

B. R. Ambedkar

> It must be recognized that there never has been a common Indian culture, that historically there have been three Indias, Brahmanic India, Buddhist India and Hindu India, each with its own culture.... It must be recognized that the history of India before the Muslim invasions is the history of a mortal conflict between Brahmanism and Buddhism. (Ambedkar 1987, 275)

Dr Bhimrao Ramji Ambedkar (1891–1956; known as 'Babasaheb' in the movement) came into politics claiming the heritage of the non-brahman movement. Between 1917–20 he returned to India after getting his degree in law in the US. He gave up service in Baroda after insults were heaped upon him as an untouchable. Settling in Bombay as a professor at Sydenham College, he associated with Shahu Maharaj of Kolhapur (notorious to nationalists as anti-brahman and pro-British) in his initial political organising. The autonomy of the dalit movement was his concern, but it was to be an autonomy in alliance with non-brahmans. At the first Depressed Classes conference in Nagpur in 1920, which he attended in the company of Shahu Maharaj, he attacked not only nationalist spokesmen, but also Vitthal Ramji Shinde, the most prominent non-dalit social reformer claiming to lead the "uplift of untouchables".

Ambedkar's emergence into politics was cautious. Very gradually he gathered a team around him, of educated and semi-educated Mahar boys, as well as a few upper-caste sympathisers, forming the Bahishkrut Hitakarni Sabha, which began to hold conferences around the province. In 1926, an explosive movement resulted when a conference at Mahad in the Konkan ended with a struggle to drink water from the town tank. The Mahad satyagraha, the first 'untouchable liberation movement', did not succeed in getting water but did end with the public burning of the Manusmruti. The campaign was partly spontaneous and partly planned; Mahad had been chosen as a place where Ambedkar had significant caste Hindu support, where a tenant movement uniting Mahar and Kunbi peasants was beginning (which developed into the biggest anti-landlord movement in Maharashtra in the 1930s), and where the municipality had already passed a resolution to open public places to untouchables.

By the time of the Simon Commission Ambedkar had clearly emerged as the most articulate dalit leader in the country with a significant mass base, and it was natural that he should be invited to the Round Table Conference. This led to the clash with Gandhi over the issue of an award of separate electorates to untouchables. For Gandhi, the integrity of Hindu society with the untouchables as its indissoluble part was a central and emotional question. The confrontation over Gandhi's fast and the Poona Pact (1932) disillusioned Ambedkar once and for all about Hindu reformism (when Gandhi undertook a fast in 1932 in protest against giving separate electorates to untouchables, Ambedkar finally gave into him; the result was the Pune pact); it inaugurated his radical period which led to an announcement in 1935 that he was "born a Hindu but would not die a Hindu" and the founding of the Independent Labour Party (ILP), a worker-peasant party with a red flag in 1936. The 'conversion announcement' set off ferment throughout the country, while the ILP went on to become the biggest opposition party in the Bombay legislative council.

With growing nationalist agitations and workers' and peasants' struggles, the 1930s was a decade of ferment. The ILP grew and became the only party in India which led struggles against capitalists and landlords along with agitations against caste oppression, calling for a radical opposition to the 'brahman-bourgeois Congress' and seeking to pull in non-brahmans as well as dalits. While Ambedkar himself did not support a non-Aryan theory of dalit-shudra identity, poems and songs published in his weekly *Janata* show how pervasive these ideas were, and how they linked anti-caste radicalism with calls for class struggle:

> *Bhils, Gonds, Dravids, their Bharat was beautiful,*
> *They were the people, the culture was theirs, the rule was theirs;*
> *The Aryas infiltrated all this, they brought their power to Bharat*
> *and Dravidans were suppressed...*
> *Brahmans, Kshatriyas, Vaishyas, all became owners*
> *Drinking the blood of slaves, making the Shudras into machines.*
> *The Brahmans, Kshatriyas and Banias got all the ownership rights.*
> *All these three call themselves brothers, they come together in times of crisis*
> *And work to split the Shudras who have become workers.*
> *"Congress", "Hindu Mahasabha", "Muslim League" are all agents of the rich,*
> *The "Independent Labour Party" is our true house...*
> *Take up the weapon of Janata*
> *Throw off the bloody magic of the owners' atrocities,*
> *Rise workers! Rise peasants! Hindustan is ours,*
> *Humanity will be built on labour,*
> *This is our birth right!*
> (Ramteke 1941)

The ILP led some major combined struggles in this period. The most notable of these was the anti-landlord agitation in the Konkan region of Maharashtra which brought together Kunbi and Mahar tenants against mainly brahman (but also some upper-caste Maratha) landlords, climaxing in a march of some 25,000 peasants to Bombay in 1938. This was followed by a massive one-day united textile workers' strike against the 'black bill' of the Congress government which outlawed strikes. Communists were involved in both of these, and at the massive peasant rally Ambedkar proclaimed, though very ambiguously, an admiration for Marxism:

> I have definitely read studiously more books on the Communist philosophy than all the Communist leaders here. However beautiful the Communist philosophy is in these books ... the test of it has

to be given in practice. And if work is done from that perspective, I feel that the labour and length of time needed to win success in Russia will not be so much needed in India.... in regard to the toilers class struggle, I feel the Communist philosophy to be closer to us. (Ramteke 1938)

The 1930s was thus the period in which Ambedkar expressed most strongly his major themes of unity and militancy: unity of workers and peasants, of dalits and non-brahmans (shudras), and unity with opposition parties against the Congress. It is striking that throughout this period (as later) it was the dominant caste peasants who were the main perpetrators of atrocities against dalits in villages, and the latter under Ambedkar fought this vigorously. Nevertheless at a broader level he called for and tried to build a unity of dalits with the Kunbi-Marathas, associated with the non-brahman party and praised Shahu Maharaj as well as Phule. Ambedkar's position here was that at the caste level, brahmanism was the main enemy, just as capitalism and landlordism were the main enemies in class terms. He consistently argued for the left and non-brahman/dalit forces to come together to form a political alternative that would fight both the Indian ruling classes and imperialism. Thus, for example, following the 1938 peasant and workers' struggles, he met with Periyar and Swami Sahajanand, the peasant leader of Bihar, in an attempt to form a broad front. Similarly, he tried to dissuade the non-brahman leaders of Maharashtra from merging their movement with the Congress, arguing that it would only make them the 'hamals' or coolies of a brahman leadership.

Yet the 1930s failed to consolidate a radical alternative to the Congress. Apart from the ability of the Congress under Gandhi to win mass support, the main barrier was the argument of the left that the main contradiction was with imperialism and that the Congress represented an 'anti-imperialist united front'. The movements dissolved, the Communists supported the British Government during the 'anti-fascist' war, and Ambedkar retreated from his radicalism to turn the ILP, which had been limited only to Maharashtra, into a much narrower but more all-India Scheduled Caste Federation (founded 1942). His goal now was to get whatever concessions he could from the British out of an independence he now saw as inevitable. He rapidly accepted a position as Labour Minister in the British government, then as Law Minister in the independent regime of Nehru. Ambedkar still saw the Congress as a 'brahman-bourgeois' party, but since there was little he could do about it he turned to reformist interest-group politics.

Ambedkar had always seen the necessity of both economic and social measures for the liberation of the dalits. But the acceptance of a mechanical Marxist framework led him to see these as separate entities and not interwoven in the way that Phule had. On the economic front, he mostly began to follow a Nehruvian-left line. While he had written two major books in the early 1920s on fiscal and monetary policy which by and large reflected a neoclassical perspective though with a severe critique of British rule, in the 1930s and 1940s he switched to a socialistic framework that took for granted the necessity of state-guided industrial development but did not confront the problem of high-caste domination over the state machinery. This was expressed in his book *States and Minorities*, written as a submission to the constitutional convention on behalf of the Scheduled Caste Federation. Economics, though, was not by this time his major concern. He was putting most of his intellectual energy into the question of the historical roots of the caste system and India's cultural identity.

Ambedkar began with a rejection not only of Marxist 'class theory' but also of the kind of 'caste theory' represented by the non-Aryan identity claims of other dalit radicals of his time. This was seen in two books published during his lifetime, *Who were the Shudras?* and *The Untouchables*. However, it was his unpublished manuscripts, *Revolution and Counter-Revolution in Ancient India* and *The Untouchables: Children of India's Ghetto* which show the breadth of his attempt to articulate a historical theory. *Revolution and Counter-Revolution* represents his major theoretical analysis, and begins with a firm rejection of the Aryan theory of caste: "The Aryans were not a race. The Aryans were a collection of people. The cement that held these together was their interest in the maintenance of a type of culture called Aryan culture" (Ambedkar 1987, 419). As he had made clear earlier:

As a matter of fact the caste system came into being long after the different races of India had commingled in blood and culture. To hold that distinctions of caste are really distinctions of race and to treat different castes as though they were so many different races is a gross perversion of the facts. What affinity is there between the Brahman of the Punjab and the Brahman of Madras? What affinity is there between the Untouchable of Bengal and the Untouchable of Madras?... The Brahman of the Punjab is racially the same stock as the Chamar of the Punjab and the Brahman of Madras is the same race as the Pariah of Madras. Caste system does not demarcate racial division. (Ambedkar 1979, 49)

It was not that Ambedkar denied 'racial' elements completely; for example, he referred to the early Magadha–Mauryan empires as being the work of 'Nagas'. He simply argued they should not be given causal priority in explaining caste. In his view, all the varnas included some kind of racial mixture; for instance the original shudras were a tribe of kshatriya Aryans who had been degraded due to conflicts with brahmans, only later being assimilated with the conquered darker-skinned non-Aryans. Similarly he rejected an analysis in terms of economic factors. In his famous phrase, somewhat similar to the way he discussed race, "caste is not a division of labour; it is a division of labourers."

Caste was thus neither racial nor economic. What then were the main explanatory factors, the motive of historical change that produced the caste system, this 'social division of the people'? With class and race rejected, and violence ignored, the emphasis is on ideological and religious factors. In Ambedkar's analysis these are interwoven as civilisational forces that produced the conflicts and changes in Indian society. Without a knowledge of the Indus valley civilisation, he differentiated three major phases, as noted above, with the central element in them being the conflict between Hinduism as representing inequalitarian and oppressive elements, and Buddhism as the advanced, egalitarian and rational mode: (1) brahmanism (the Vedic period, basically tribal in nature and characterised by varna among the Vedic Aryans, though this was not based on birth); (2) the 'revolutionary' period of Buddhism, marked by the rise of the Magadha and Mauryan states and bringing about a great advance in the status of women and shudras whose position had become degraded in the last stages of the Vedic period; and (3) the 'counter-revolutionary' period of Hinduism marked by the Manusmruti, the transformation of varna into caste, and the complete downgrading of shudras and women (Ambedkar 1987, 316–17).

> The triumphant Brahmanism began an onslaught on both the Shudras and the women in pursuit of the old idea, namely servility, and Brahmanism did succeed in making the Shudras and the women the servile classes: Shudras the serfs to the three higher classes and the women the serfs to their husbands. Of the black deeds committed by Brahmanism after its triumph over Buddhism this one is the blackest. There is no parallel in history for so foul deeds of degradation committed by a class of usurpers in the name of class domination. (Ibid., 336)

It has to be noted here that in using the term 'shudra' Ambedkar was clearly not referring to the untouchables, whom he saw as 'broken men' settled outside the villages; he was referring to the non-brahman masses whom he saw, along with untouchables and tribals, as victims of the caste system. By the 1940s, however, his hope that there would be a unified struggle was at a low ebb, and he was in his political writings treating "Hindus" as a "majority" that included non-brahmans and was posed against such minorities as Muslims and dalits.

Nevertheless, Ambedkar's longer-term strategy was to break up that majority, to dissolve Hinduism itself, and do so by building a unity of dalits and middle castes (non-brahmans) which would be both a caste and a class unity of peasants and workers, against the brahman-bourgeois Congress. The last years of his life saw a return to this kind of united front, expressed in the change of his Scheduled Caste Federation into the (hopefully non-caste) Republican Party. It participated in the Samyukta Maharashtra Samiti, organised to fight for a Marathi-speaking state and which was actually the first full left-democratic front of opposition parties. Ambedkar, in fact, had argued that the united front should continue even after the winning of a Marathi-speaking state, and fight for the interests of the rural poor; and a massive land satyagraha led by his lieutenant

Dadasaheb Gaikwad and communist peasant leaders followed in both 1956 and 1965.

Yet, the end of Ambedkar's life is remembered by the innumerable number of dalit followers neither for the class unity of peasants and workers, nor for the renewed effort at forming the Republican Party as a broad-based organisation, but for his conversion to Buddhism along with nearly a million dalits in Nagpur. For Ambedkar, and for the militant dalits who followed him, Hinduism, in the final analysis, remained a religion of caste that had to be renounced and destroyed if the masses of India were to win liberation. He had written in 1936, in confrontation with Gandhi and Punjab anti-caste radicals, that it was necessary to deal with religion. Indian socialists, he noted:

> will be compelled to take account of caste after the revolution
> if (they) do not take account of it before revolution. This is only
> another way of saying that, turn in any direction you like, caste is
> the monster that crosses your path. You cannot have political reform,
> you cannot have economic reform, unless you kill this monster.
> (Ambedkar 1979, 47)

But this, he went on to argue, required that "you must destroy the Religion of the Shrutis and the Shastras. Nothing else will succeed (Ibid., 75–77)." "You will succeed in saving Hinduism if you kill brahmanism," he argued, softening his blow with suggested reforms for Hinduism. It is perhaps this kind of language that has provided a thin wedge for the BJP to try to co-opt even Ambedkar as a 'Hindu reformer'. But such Hindu reformism would have required the rejection of all the sacred books of the Hindus, of Rama and Krishna as ideals, and in the end Ambedkar was unwilling to believe this was possible. His unpublished writings are harsh in their overall critique:

> Is there then no principle in Hinduism [to] which all Hindus, no
> matter what their other differences are, feel bound to render willing
> obedience? It seems to me there is, and that principle is the principle
> of caste. (Ambedkar 1987, 336)

The way to liberation, then, involved economic and ideological struggle, and Ambedkar never gave up the former. His stress, however, was on ideological/cultural struggle, and though he could not succeed in fully integrating it with an economic alternative, he gave it a sharpness that would remain the challenge before socialists—to deal with the "monster that would always cross their path", the issue of caste and its religious justifications.

Eight

Hinduism as Delhi Rule

Periyar and the National Question

As the colonial period drew to an end the surface waves of Indian politics were dominated by the issue of Muslim separatism and Hindu identity. Hinduism came to be a taken-for-granted identity, whether it was the moderate and liberal version most Congressmen subscribed to, or the increasingly virulent form of Hindu nationalism. The latter, growing throughout the 1920s and 1930s, began to increasingly emphasise not only blood and territory (race, religion and nation) but also language, projecting Sanskrit/Hindi as the quintessentially 'Indian' languages. This had a significant north Indian bias. *Hindi-Hindu-Hindustan*, the emotive slogan of north Indian fundamentalism, had a powerful negative side: the equation of language, religion and nation encouraged not only those with a different religious identity but also those with a separate linguistic identity to see themselves as a different 'nation'. Thus, the other side of the powerful centralising tendency of Hindu fundamentalism was that many anti-caste movements turned to a regional and anti-northern, as well as anti-brahman identification.

Caste is not ethnicity, and Ambedkar above all was to insist on this distinction and take a resolutely all-Indian, even centralist attitude. But caste, community and ethnicity have common features, also seen in the vernacular meanings of jati and quaum, which are often overlapping. From the time of Phule a broad stream in the anti-caste movement had stressed these, seeing the brahmanic elites as Aryan and themselves as non-Aryan, of a different ethnic community and even a different race. Given the diversity of India, reflected especially in the diversity of the non-brahman and dalit communities, it is not surprising that these mass ethnic identities got expressed in different forms in different regions. The opposition to 'brahman' and 'Hindu' then got reflected in varying non-Hindi and sometimes anti-north Indian nationality identifications.

By the 1930s, for example, Sikh and Muslim religious identities were also taking on regional/nationalist aspects and in the process opposed Congress domination as Hindu domination and 'brahman-bania rule'. The caste discourse of the opposition helped to link them to the non-brahman and dalit movements and perhaps provided a ground for the alliances that were taking place. In the 1930s for instance, Mangoo Ram of the Punjab allied with the Unionist Party and the Namashudras with the Krishak Praja Party in Bengal. At the same time the strong Hindu-Muslim antagonisms which were developing especially in north India were, . in many other regions getting diversified into demands for regional separation and autonomy. By the late 1940s the movement for Pakistan was feeding that for Dravidistan and similar trends could be seen elsewhere. Anti-Hinduism was taking on a rather complex, anti-northern, anti-centralist character.

Developments in Tamil Nadu provide an insight into the process. Here was a strongly independent Dravidian linguistic identity and a long history of being the southern centre of the subcontinent, not only unconquered by northerners but a centre of empires of its own, stretching sometimes overseas and oriented in many ways more towards south-east Asia in contrast to the northern west Asian linkages. Here, since the late nineteenth century, anti-brahmanism had the built-in claim of being the non-Aryan original inhabitants of the land. This led to an idealisation of ancient Tamil society; Saivaism, or the Saiva Siddhanta philosophy was posed as an indigenous, even non-Hindu religion. This was to form the basis for claiming an identity as Dravidians and, by the 1940s and 1950s for Tamil nationalism.

The first anti-caste movement in Tamil Nadu was neither particularly ethnic-oriented; it was rather religious in orientation and it was led by a dalit, a Pariyar Siddha physician, Pandit Iyothee Thass. He had formed, at the turn of the century, the Sakya Buddhist Society or South Indian Buddhist League, based mainly on dalits but drawing in many intellectuals from other caste groups. In many ways this movement was a forerunner of Ambedkar's Buddhism. Iyothee Thass interpreted ancient India as Buddhist India; like Phule, he saw an original, peaceful and prosperous society overwhelmed and conquered by Aryans imposing their brahmanic ideology and caste social system. Iyothee Thass developed his perspective independently, and more than Phule he saw the process as pioneered by deception rather than violence. To him the dalits of Tamil Nadu were 'casteless Indians' or 'casteless Tamilians', descendents of Buddha's clan, the Sakyas.

The non-brahman movement which arose in the 1920s in Tamil Nadu, however, ignored these contributions of Iyothee Thass and was more elite-based than in Maharashtra with the relatively high-caste Vellalas and other non-brahman landlords and professionals from the Telugu and Malayalam speaking regions able to confront the brahmans on their own footing, increasingly without having to build much of a mass movement (see Irshick 1969; also see Geetha and Rajadurai 1993). Their political party, the South Indian Liberal Association, was the most successful of the non-brahman parties in India in the Legislative Council in the 190s.

But, by the 1920s a new, militant, mass-oriented movement arose. Its leader was E. V. Ramaswami, 'Periyar' (1879–1973), from a merchant family of Erode. He had joined the Congress in 1919, then gradually became disillusioned with what he saw as its brahmanic leadership. In the early 1920s he took part in the Vaikom temple satyagraha, reportedly clashing with Gandhi while taking a militant position. He later argued that Gandhi had pushed him out of the satyagraha when he engineered a compromise. Nonetheless, Periyar returned to Tamil Nadu as the 'hero of Vaikom'. He subsequently clashed with Congress leaders over a proposed resolution for reservations in legislatures for non-brahmans and untouchables. In 1925, Periyar left the Congress. In 1927, during a tour of south India, Gandhi defended varnashrama dharma and Periyar contested this hotly, in personal meetings and in articles in his journal *Kudi Arasu*. He now claimed that three conditions were necessary for the country to gain its freedom: destruction of the Congress, of the so-called Hindu religion, and of brahman domination (see Murugesan and Subramanyam 1975, 64).

Periyar formed the Self-Respect League in 1926 and its first conference was held in 1929. This movement spread across Tamil Nadu. Its focus was similar to that of Phule's Satyashodhak Samaj, opposing brahman priesthood, calling for the abolition of caste, and supporting the liberation of women. He attacked all religions more than Phule did, taking an atheistic stance that contrasted with the modified Saivaism of the non-brahman elite:

> *There is no god,*
> *there is no god,*
> *there is no god at all.*
> *He who invented god is a fool.*
> *He who propagates god is a scoundrel.*
> *He who worships god is a barbarian.*

The dialectic between Phule's theism and Periyar's atheism was in a sense duplicated in the small state of Kerala where Narayanaswami Guru's 'one religion, one caste, one god' was opposed by his atheistic disciple Ayyapan with the slogan 'no religion, no caste and no god for mankind'. The radical nationalism of the Self-Respect Movement inspired many at the time, among them the poet Bharati Dasan who published his first collection in 1938 which invoked 'original' Tamil values not as in the sense of seeking a revivalistic return to a golden age but as an inspiration for an autonomous modernity:

> *Is it greatness to refuse the right of women*
> *Or is it great to be happy with the progress of women?*
> *Is it right that women marry out of love,*
> *Or is it right that we kill them after performing a child marriage?*
> *Is it right to believe in the Vedas, in God, in all this decay?*
> *Or is it right to establish socialism on earth?*

Will we live continuing the divisions which surround us?
Or will we live rising up through self-respect?
(Quoted in Irschick 1986, 224–25)

Bharati Dasan's socialism reflected a new radicalism and a temporary coming together of anti-caste and class themes in the early 1930s. On the one hand, Periyar's equalitarianism, anti-caste radicalism and atheism, all expressed in powerful Tamil speeches, were attracting a group of militant lower-caste youth, giving a new invigoration to the old non-brahman movement and radicalising it. On the other hand, a sparking role was played by Singaravelu, a union leader from a fish workers' caste who is considered the 'first Communist of south India'. He had been another of the associates of Iyothee Thass' Sakya Buddhism, and was also the first Indian to independently form a labour party, considered a forerunner of the Communist Party (see Murugesan and Subrammanyam 1975).

In 1932, Periyar toured the Soviet Union and was impressed by the concrete accomplishments of atheistic socialism while Singaravelu wrote a series of articles in *Kudi Arasu* expounding socialism and a materialistic interpretation of history. On Periyar's return, he and Singaravelu placed a new programme before Self-Respect activists in December 1932 and it was suggested that a political party be formed, using the name Samadharma party as the closest Tamil equivalent to 'socialism'. Socialism now began to be propagated from Self-Respect platforms, while anti-landlord and anti-moneylender conferences were held by non-brahman activists.

But this coming together of the left and anti-caste movements seemed doomed from the beginning. On the one hand conservatives in the non-brahman movement opposed it, and when in 1933 Periyar was arrested and jailed, it was clear that British pressure was on. On the other hand, Communist leaders, centred in Bombay, regarded any dilution of a class line with suspicion. Singaravelu's type of indigenous socialism, identified with dangerous non-class forces such as the anti-caste movement and regional-national identities, had to be kept under a tight rein. By 1934, Singaravelu, then in his seventies, began to argue that the term Samadharma should be dropped and the movement openly identify itself as socialist. The real split, though, was on a straightforward political issue: whether, in the 1934 elections, with no socialist party around, the Self-Respect movement should support the Justice Party or the Congress. Periyar saw his political future in a revival and radicalisation of the Justice Party. The left could see it only in the Congress, which by 1935 they were identifying explicitly as the 'anti-imperialist united front'. In 1936, the Communist leadership ordered Singaravelu and others to dissolve their organisation and instead join the Congress Socialist Party, a part of the solidly all-Indian National Congress within which the Communists were working. Dange's speech at the conference which dissolved the movement stressed the dangers of linguistic nationalism: "He reminded the conference that not only Tamil Nadu but the whole of India is under British imperialist domination, and that unless the bondage of India under British imperialism is destroyed on an all-India scale it is impossible even to dream of socialism" (Ibid., 83).

The result of young radical communist cadres leaving the movement was to deprive it of a class thrust. As Periyar and his co-workers clashed with the 'brahmanic' left, they increasingly identified with a linguistic nationalism. In the south it was easy to give a specific ethnic and national identity to non-Aryan: the people obviously had a language with a non-European origin and the original inhabitants were Dravidian or Tamil. Phule had attacked the story of Vishnu's avatars as representing an external, Aryan conquest of the subcontinent; Periyar described it as a conquest of the south by the north. Phule had taken Bali Raja, the mythological 'peasant king', as a hero; the Tamils took Ravana as the symbol of the south. In this they were only following popular Ramayana traditions. Ravana is seen as hero in many non-Valmiki versions of the epic in south and west India, south east Asia and even Kashmir. The versions emphasise love and war, the heroism and tragic fate of Ravana, in contrast to the feudal, patriarchal and hierarchical values emphasised by the Chinese and north Indian versions centred around Rama.

By the 1940s, Tamil/Dravidian nationalistic themes were coming to dominate opposition politics. In 1936 a Congress government (headed by Rajagopalacharya) came to power in Madras Province as in most parts of India. As Congress began what Sumit Sarkar has described as "a steady shift to the Right, occasionally veiled by 'Left' rhetoric" (Sarkar 1983, 351), organisations of peasants and workers went on the offensive in many parts of the country. In Madras as well, strikes and campaigns took place, but the split between Periyar and the communists meant that there was no coordination of the class-caste struggle, not even a search for a common ground. Periyar himself was hardly an ideologue, and took only passing interest in economic issues. Without socialist cadres to push him on, he began to organise constant campaigns against the imposition of Hindi, stressing the theme of Dravidian/Tamil nationality. With the rise of the demand for Pakistan the movement gained strength, and in 1939 the Dravida Nadu Conference for the Advocacy of a Separate and Independent Dravidastan, demanded a separate country along the lines of Pakistan (Diehl 1977, 62).

Regional nationalism was beginning to grow in various parts of India. The demand for Pakistan itself was from the beginning conceived not simply in religious terms but in religious-territorial terms identified with the north-west: the earliest version spoke of 'Pakistan, Hindustan and Bengal', and the one proposed in 1938–39 included Hyderabad to make up four independent states. By the 1940s Jinnah was willing to include Dravidastan as one of the four regions (Moore 1990). The 1938–39 proposal reflected a vigorous campaign in Hyderabad sponsored by the Nizam to promote a composite Hindu-Muslim 'Deccani' culture as a basis for identity. This could win over a few prominent dalit leaders, though it was ultimately compromised by its association with a feudal regime and could withstand neither Hindu nor Muslim fundamentalism.

Similarly, Sikh/Punjabi identity was expressing itself both in regional and religious terms, by sharing with the non-brahmans an antagonism towards brahmans and banias. In Kashmir, Muslim Kashmiris were beginning to conceptualise their identity not simply in religious but in regional/ethnic terms, as 'Kashmiriat' Even in the far north-east, the educated Assamese stressed an anti-Bengali identity while identifying with Hinduism (Vaishnavism); the tribals of the plains were questioning both Assamese high-caste identification and asserting a specific north-eastern identity. This identity carried the sense of being Mongoloid in contrast with the Aryan identities of high-caste Assamese Hindus as well as Muslims. The first convention of the All-Assam Tribes and Races Federation· in 1945 unanimously resolved that:

> In view of the fact that historically, Assam proper, with its hills, was never a part or province of India and that its people, particularly the Tribes and Races inhabiting it are ethnically and culturally different from the people of the rest of India, this convention is emphatically opposed to Assam proper with its hills being included into any proposed division of India, Pakistan or Hindustan, and demands that it should be constituted into a separate Free State into which the Hill Districts bordering Assam be incorporated. (Cited in Phukon 1986)

'Subnational' identities were thus becoming a major undercurrent of politics in the 1940s. They did not, it should be noted, always imply a separatist nationalism; this was more likely in the border areas. Such identities could also lead to demands for autonomy coupled with a loose federal centre. Thus, for instance, the leader of the Unionist Party in the Punjab, Sikandar Hayat Khan, rejected Pakistan as the equivalent of a 'Muslim raj' and suggested instead a three-tier structure with autonomous provinces grouped into seven regions—these joined in a loose confederation in which the centre had charge only over defence, external affairs, currency and customs (Sarkar 1983, 378–80). This type of autonomy was to be the demand with which Sheikh Abdullah's National Conference agreed to Kashmir joining the Indian Union; and it was to be revived after independence in both Punjab and Kashmir—intermittently with movements for independent states.

Meanwhile Periyar had decided to focus on the question of India's future and succeeded in building a political organisation that would become the major party in Tamil Nadu. In 1944, he revived the Justice Party, changed its name to Dravida Kazhagham (DK) and declared its goal to be a 'sovereign, independent Dravidian Republic'. The flag adopted was black with a red circle. Independence was declared a 'day of mourning' for representing the enslavement of the southerners (Diehl 1977, 62–63). Several strands were brought together by the DK with their focal point being Tamil nationalism:

We want our country;
Change the name to Tamil Nadu;
All-India Union Government means a government
protecting Hindu religion;
We must leave the Hindu Delhi.
(Ibid., 63)

Tamil nationalism, linked with the anti-caste movement, thus became a powerful force in the south. However it could win none of its major demands. The post-independence Congress government succeeded in diluting the radicalism of the Dravidian forces. The DK gave birth to the Dravida Munnetra Kazhagam (DMK) which gave up the separatist demand, and then to the All-India Anna Dravida Munnetra Kazhagam (AIADMK) which capitalised on the charisma of its superstar leader and asserted an all-India identity, allied with Congress and eventually propped up its dead hero's film star companion as a temperamental dictatorial leader. The major problem of the Dravidian movement remained the difficulty of winning dalit support—something Phule had put at the centre of his strategy. In Tamil Nadu, it was not the radical Ambedkar but the Hindu Mahasabhaite M. C. Rajah who was the most well-known dalit leader, and his alienation from the Dravidian movement was the other side of the distancing of the movement itself from dalits. The south thus witnessed a powerful non-brahman movement and a strong opposition to 'Hinduism' but more than in any other region was plagued by splits between communists and Dravidians, and dalits and non-brahmans.

The currents of regional or subnational (linguistic national) identity were thus significant during the colonial period. They overlapped in complicated ways with claims to a non-Hindu religious identity, but they nearly always shared a framework of opposition to a brahman-bania, Delhi-based centralised rule. The logical outcome of these movements was not necessarily towards the establishment of an independent nation-state; demands for independence were often raised, but the thrust was just as much on a decentralised, federal structure with much more autonomous regions than in the Indian union which came into existence. The triumph of the Congress finally represented both a triumph of a 'Hindu' identity and of a centralised, Delhi-based state in the Indian subcontinent.

Nine

Independent India

Brahmanic Socialism, Brahmanic Globalisation

During the colonial period the overwhelmingly brahman Indian elite fashioned an upgraded 'Hinduism' which reinterpreted Indian identity and Indian history in a way that could draw low castes, women, adivasis and others into a 'national community' whose core was conceived to be the Vedic, Aryan, brahmanic tradition. Whether it was Tilak and the Ganapati festival, Vivekananda and Ramakrishna, or Dayananda and the Arya Samaj, largely high-caste symbols were used to define the heart of this tradition. Even after Hindutva theorists began to argue that the Aryans actually originated in the subcontinent, the notion of Aryans as a core group was kept. And, while the militant 'Hindu nationalists' of the RSS and Hindu Mahasabha gave this a more virulent anti-Muslim character by making Hinduism the centre of the Indian state, there were disturbing similarities between their imaging of Indian history and that of proclaimed secularists such as Nehru or even Dange.

While continuing to use such emotive Hindu terminology as Ram Raj and identifying himself fully with this tradition, Gandhi nevertheless sought to give it a major reinterpretation by proclaiming non-violence and truth as its core. He also offered the basis for a different path of development with his notion of *gram swaraj* and a decentralised, village-centred economy. But this was so inextricably linked with Ram Raj and the anti-technological and anti-sexual ideas of limiting wants, as to discredit it among those—like Ambedkar—concerned with rationality and a need to lift Indians out of their current, colonially-induced poverty.

In the end Gandhi fell a victim to the Hindu nationalists themselves who were furious at what they saw as his responsibility for Partition. Yet, ironically, contemporary 'revisionist' historical scholarship is stressing the role of the Congress leadership in choosing Partition, since a united India would inevitably have been a decentralised and federated one giving too many concessions to the Muslim-majority areas and only a truncated India could offer the centralised state structure they demanded (Roy 1991).

Forces countering the Hindu majority interpretation of Indian society and history existed throughout the colonial period, pre-dating the overriding preoccupation with the 'Muslim problem'. This is clearly shown in the work of Jotiba Phule. But these forces were fragmented and remained subordinated. The Communists themselves who claimed to be the main 'class' opposition to the 'bourgeois' Congress could not offer a serious challenge at the level of mass mobilisation, despite their considerable working class base and such sporadic tempests as the Telengana revolt. Worse, they never even tried to counter its Hinduist interpretation of history, with the most well known Communist excursion into historical interpretation, Dange's *India: From Primitive Communism to Slavery*, also beginning with the Aryans. The non-brahman/Satyashodhak movement in Maharashtra was absorbed in the 1930s; that in Tamil Nadu evolved into a more long-lasting Dravidian movement but one which was even more split from left and dalit trends. The radical voices of early feminists were buried under the weight of a more compromising and upper-class pre-independence women's movement. The peripheries, such as the north-east, remained remote, without influence on 'all India' developments. In this context, the dalit movement from the 1920s sought to carry on a cultural and economic challenge to the dominant elite, but the efforts of leaders like Ambedkar and numerous others throughout the country had no hopes of achieving hegemony on their own, without the basic shudra-ati-shudra unity which Phule had projected and which Ambedkar also wished to build.

It was the Congress which triumphed. The usual categorisation of the Congress by the left, as representing some form of 'bourgeois' (national, monopoly, comprador) or 'bourgeois-landlord' force, simply misses much reality. Ambedkar's 'bourgeois-brahman' or more aptly bourgeois (bania)-bureaucratic (brahman) would be more accurate. With the assassination of Gandhi marking the end of an era of struggle, the suave and sophisticated Nehru was the natural leader of the party. With the Second Five-Year Plan, a 'socialist pattern of development'—a focus on heavy industrialisation and the state sector—was chosen. This was influenced by the powerful successes claimed by the Soviet Union, by the overwhelming swing of all newly independent countries towards state-controlled development, and by a consensus even among 'development economists' on such issues. But the 'Nehru model' had its specific Hindu character from the beginning. As Nehru himself described the choice of socialism over capitalism:

> The old culture managed to live through many a fierce storm and tempest, but, though it kept its outer form, it lost its real content. Today it is fighting silently and desperately against a new and all-powerful opponent—the *bania* civilization of the capitalist West. It will succumb to this newcomer, for the West brings science and science brings food for the hungry millions. But the West also brings an antidote to the evils of this cut-throat civilization—the principles of socialism for cooperation, and service to the community for the common good. This is not so unlike the old Brahman ideal of service, but it means the brahmanization (not in the religious sense, of course) of all classes and groups and the abolition of class distinctions. It may be that when India puts on her new garment, as she must, for the old is torn and tattered, she will have it cut in this fashion, so as to make it conform both to present conditions and her old thought. (Nehru 1941, 274–75)

The left's critique of Congress socialism has been that it was capitalist reformism because it did not admit of working class leadership. This is insufficient. It was worse than that. It was brahmanism, of course idealised by Nehru in terms of 'service' and 'cooperation', but with a clear implication that these meant management; socialism was identified with planning and the public sector, with statism. That it could mean something very different, the rule of the shudras (the working classes), never seems to have occurred to Nehru. The only thing he had against the Gandhian notion of 'trusteeship', apparently, was that it could be that of private capitalists, the hated banias. Brahmanic trusteeship in the hands of a public sector was another matter.

Gandhi had opposed a heavy industrially-powered development, arguing that "by using Manchester cloth we only waste our money; but by reproducing Manchester in India we save our money at the price of our blood because our very moral being will be sapped" (in Iyer 1986, 257). "Reproducing Manchester", only under state ownership, was precisely what India's new ruling elite set out to do. Neither Gandhi nor any of the well-known Gandhian economists could offer a rational basis for a decentralised development; Gandhism remained at the moral level, and efforts to promote khadi and village industries remained a matter of government patronage which had little to do with real self reliance. Industrialisation was a goal no third world country rejected; and the overwhelming consensus of development theory at the time of Indian independence made the Nehru-Mahalanobis type of planning and the focus on the public sector practically inevitable. But the costs of the path not taken were borne by a major section of the toiling people whose poverty remained as oppressive as ever.

The brahmanic socialism of the Nehruvian model of development created a powerful superstructure—a heavy industrial base, a scientific and technological establishment, an extensive university system, a glittering cultural scene. The growth rate it involved, aptly nicknamed the 'Hindu rate of growth' by economist Raj Krishna was, at 3.5 per cent, quite respectable by the previous history of economic growth but was barely 1.5 per cent per capita annually in the first three decades after independence: it rose slightly in the 1980s so that the per capita growth rate was 1.9 per cent from 1965–1990. But this was significantly lower than the 2.9 per cent for all other low income countries and 5.8 per cent for China in the same period. As the South Commission put it,

Growth was not high enough to trickle down.... in India, growth in the first three post-war decades was much slower than the average for the developing countries. The rise in India's per capita income, of the order of about 1.5 per cent per year, was too small to secure a significant improvement in the living standards of the masses of the people. (*The Challenge to the South* 1992, 84–85; also see IBRD 1992, Table I, 218–19)

Because of the stress on import-substitution using capital-intensive measures, insufficient industrial employment was generated, and most of the burden was borne by agriculture. The primary sector, mainly agriculture, which had employed an estimated 75 per cent of the population producing 54 per cent of national income at the end of British rule (Lal 1988, 221), was still, by 1991, employing 67 per cent of the workforce, but its share of GDP had come down to 31 per cent meaning in effect that nearly as many in agriculture were getting a much smaller proportion of the total income (*Census of India* 1991; *World Development Report* 1992, Table 2). This immiserated primary sector threw off its surplus labour, the large majority of them not getting well-protected jobs in factories but becoming the growing 'unorganised sector' living in slums in cities and small towns.

In terms of human welfare this meant that the islands of growth in industry and agriculture did not result in significant welfare gains for the majority. The average lifespan rose to 58 for women and 60 for men by 1990, a significant gain from 44 and 46 respectively in 1965 and from the drastic situation of the colonial period when life expectancy did not reach 30 until 1941. But it was a stunted and undernourished population surviving on an average of only 2229 calories per day (*World Development Report* 1992, Table 28, 273–74; Table 22, 280–81) and India remains the only major country in the world where women continue to live shorter lives than men. Between 1980 and 1990, as an international survey on hunger showed, 41 per cent of children below four years of age were classified as underweight and 30 per cent of babies were born with low birth weights. Twenty per cent of the population even in the 1980s were without access to health facilities; 24 per cent of the urban and 50 per cent of the rural population were without access to safe water; and 28 per cent of urban and 40 per cent of the rural population were classified as below an absolute poverty level (*Hunger 1992*, Tables 2 and 3, 180–83). By the World Bank's figures, in absolute numbers, there were 420 million poor and 250 million 'extremely poor'; of the poor, 77 per cent were estimated to be rural (*World Development Report, 1990; Poverty*, 31). This was, according to the World Bank, a decline since 1972, but sheer numbers still made India the poorest country in the world, housing over one-third of the world's poor.

This was a far cry from the dreams, of both India's freedom fighters, who had fought not only for independence but also for prosperity and equality, and of the dalit and non-brahman critics who had insisted above all on equality. As the crisis of the late 1960s deepened, pressures for change grew. Tentative liberalisation moves in the 1980s were followed by a full-fledged 'new economic policy' of the 1990s. The country moved into a new era of 'liberalization, privatization and globalization', LPG, the mantra of the bourgeoisie.

Trade was liberalised; foreign capital was given greater scope; the rupee was made to float freely on the international market; huge, inefficient public sector companies began to be sold off. Gradually the license-permit raj was, in part, dismantled. The 'Hindu rate of growth' began to give way to a new thrust for rapid economic growth. India began to be seen as a world economic power, one of the 'new tigers' roaming in the globalised jungles of the world.

Partly this can be seen as a struggle between two sections of the ruling class—a mainly bania set of industrial capitalists (along with some very brahmanic firms in the IT sector) and the brahman-dominated bureaucracy. The 'Hindu rate of growth' began to change; it rose to 9 and 10 per cent. The stock market zoomed. Even with a world recession developing from late 2008, it continued to zoom. Part of the reason was that 'black money' from the world over was getting parked in India as the world economic leaders decided to close off the small island 'tax havens' where it had been earlier kept; but India's own home market seemed quite solid. In some ways, it was a 'shining India'.

But the same inequalities remained which had been part of the earlier, more stagnant, statist era. In contrast to the earlier South Commission assessment, growth was high enough to trickle down, but it was barely a trickle. India remained very low on all human rights indicators, even in contrast to other developing countries. Poverty declined, but rather minimally. Millions still faced hunger; farmers committed suicide as agriculture remained backward and discriminated against under a liberal trade regime as much as under a statist one.

If anything, caste tensions increased with growth. The earlier 'brahmanic socialism' phase had led to an argument by some that the 'Hindu rate of growth' was necessarily low because higher growth would cause turmoil in the society. Higher growth with increasing inequality did indeed lead to turmoil. The first crisis in the mid 1960s had led to an upsurge of radicalism in the seventies, including naxalism and anti-caste organising. By the 1990s, dalits and OBCs—'other backward castes', the new name for the ex-shudras, deriving from the Mandal Commission—were organising in new ways, representing a challenge to Hindutva, brahmanic globalisation and social-economic inequalities. It is to this, that we now turn.

Ten

Hinduism as Feudal Backwardness
The Dalit Panthers

The present Congress rule is essentially a continuation of the old Hindu feudalism which kept the dalits deprived of power, wealth and status for thousands of years.... the entire state machinery is dominated by the feudal interests, who for thousands of years, under religious sanctions, controlled all the wealth and power, who today own most of the agricultural land industry, economic resources and all other instruments of power....

Who is a dalit?   Members of scheduled castes and tribes, neo-Buddhists, the working people, the landless and poor peasants, women and all those who are being exploited politically, economically and in the name of religion.

Who are our friends?   Revolutionary parties set to break down the caste system and class rule. Left parties that are left in a true sense. All other sections of society that are suffering due to economic and political oppression.

Who are our enemies?   Power, wealth, price. Landlords, capitalists, moneylenders and their lackeys. Those parties who indulge in religious or casteist politics and the government which depends on them...

We do not want a little place in Brahman Alley. We want the rule of the whole land. We are not looking at persons but a system. Change of heart, liberal education, etc., will not end our state of exploitation. When we gather a revolutionary mass, rouse the people, out of the struggle of this giant mass will come the tidal wave of revolution. (Joshi 1984, 141–46)

So ran the manifesto of the Dalit Panthers, a militant organisation of dalit youth. Born in Bombay in 1972, with its leadership drawn from a new generation of young poets and writers, and founded against the backdrop of increasing rural and urban tensions. It was a period in which atrocities against dalits in the villages, often of brutal and horrifying forms, seemed on the increase.

- In Maharashtra, the Dalit Panthers sparked a whole new political wave, fighting the Shiv Sena, energising dalits, attempting to organise efforts throughout the country.
- In Karnataka, a dispute over a cultural issue (a dalit minister was forced to resign after describing conventional Kannada literature as "cattle feed") led to widespread clashes throughout the state between dalits and caste Hindus. The dalits raised the slogan, "Throw the brahmans into the gutter along with the Gita" and eventually formed the Dalit Sangharsh Samiti with branches all over the state.
- In Bihar, a revived Naxalite movement sprang up among the dalits, with issues of honour or *izzat* (mainly the protection of dalit women against landlord molestation) and agricultural wages being central.
- In Tamil Nadu, Ambedkarite organisations began to be founded in many villages.

Other areas were slower to pick up the cue: a Dalit Panther unit was formed in Gujarat in 1980 after widespread upper-caste rioting in protest against reservations; an Andhra Dalit Mahasabha was formed in 1984 after a brutal massacre of dalits in the village of Karamchedu. Whatever its form in each region, a new movement was enveloping most of the country, and the question 'will the caste war turn into a class war?' almost began to replace the more conventional, 'will the Green Revolution turn into a red one?'

Efforts were also underway to give a new theoretical articulation to the class-caste struggle. This question was taken up by V. T. Rajshekar of Bangalore, the founder-editor of *Dalit Voice* and though he swung fairly quickly to an emphasis almost solely on caste struggle, his articulate, aggressive and often vitriolic journalism won him readers throughout the country and among dalits abroad. *Dalit Voice* survived as a small near-weekly publication, and was for decades a major English outlet for expression of views and themes by dalits and OBCs throughout India. It provided vigorous polemics, sought to woo Muslims, attacked imperialism, and sometimes showed execrably bad taste.

A more Marxist attempt at integration was made by Sharad Patil, a district organiser of the CPI(M) in the tribal belt of Maharashtra. He took time off from his party work to study Sanskrit as a basis for a theoretical interpretation of Indian history, produced a new approach, 'Marxism-Phule-Ambedkarism' and then a new party, the Satyashodhak Communist Party. The party attracted a wave of young cadre, and though after some time they split from Sharad Patil, whose authoritarianism was sometimes hard to take, they continued to follow his thematic views. Patil wrote several books, beginning with *Das-Shudra Slavery*, published in both Marathi and English, attempting to outline a history of India from his 'Maphuaa' perspective.

In Andhra, Kancha Ilaiah began to theorise the role of both patriarchy and caste. Ilaiah, a scholar from a low-caste herding community, had experienced discrimination in his own life; including in the Naxalite-leaning civil liberties movement. His first book, *Why I am not a Hindu*, proclaimed proudly that the dalits and ex-shudra communities had different deities, different ways of life, different production systems from the upper castes. He described them as the "productive castes" in contrast to the parasitical "twice-born" communities. He went on to write of Buddhism, proclaimed "buffalo nationalism" (why was the cow sacred? It was white, found in Europe—in contrast to the common buffalo, much more productive in milk, an Asiatic and black animal), and talked of a "post-Hindu" India.

Theory almost inevitably led to political action. Though the Panthers themselves were born in the context of a great disillusionment with the traditional Ambedkarite Republican Party, and even leaped to fame with an electoral boycott in 1974 that significantly benefited the communist candidate in the heart of Bombay's working class area, the thrust of the movement took them into electoral as well as revolutionary politics. One of the most important of the new parties was founded by a Punjabi dalit, Kanshi Ram, who had been turned into an Ambedkarite after his experiences in Maharashtra; a theme we will take up in the next chapter. Kanshi Ram avoided the Panthers and the more flashy dalit agitations of the time, and began with an organisation of dalit, backward caste and minority government employees. He developed this by 1980 into the Bahujan Samaj Party, with its base mainly in north and north-west India and an ability to cut drastically into the taken-for-granted 'vote banks' of the Congress. Another was the Bharatiya Republican Party, founded at almost the same time by Prakash Ambedkar, the grandson of Dr Ambedkar. With the Buddhist revival, and a wave of conversions to Islam that was overplayed by the Hindutva forces to stress a 'danger to Hinduism', the new ferment was clearly covering all aspects of social life.

The Panthers had been the starting point of this ferment and their thrust was to universalise the dalit identity as proletarian experience. This differentiated it from the dalit movement of Ambedkar's time, which had accepted the separation of economic and cultural spheres, of class and caste, sometimes ignoring the economic sphere substantially. It also contrasted with the first new left upsurge in India, the Naxalite revolt, with its rural orientation and Maoist fervour for agrarian revolution. Now, after the Naxalites had been crushed (at least temporarily) in Bombay, the bastion of Indian capitalism itself, economic exploitation and cultural oppression intertwined to define a new dalit revolt— linked in imagery if not in terms of a concrete socio-economic analysis.

Many factors brought about the Dalit Panther phenomenon: the economic crisis which had been unfolding since the middle 1960s, the disillusionment with the history of corruption and co-opting of the party founded by Ambedkar; the spread of education; and the nature of the capitalist city as a communications centre. It is true, of course to say that the poets and activists of the dalit movement were 'petty bourgeois' or 'middle class'; but what was striking was the changing nature of this middle class and its increased spread. In Ambedkar's time this consisted of only a very small section of educated dalits who could provide the core of activists for a movement; by the 1970s education and the gains from reservations had produced a widespread section. It ranged upwards to a few high-level government employees and political leaders and downwards to the villages, where in most areas some minimal education of the boys of the most conscious dalit castes (Mahars, Chambhars, etc.) was practically universal and was slowly beginning to include the girls as well. The nature of the Indian education system made them vulnerable to the modernistic upgradings of Hindu ideologies found in school books; but simultaneously the ability to read and write proved a powerful weapon for the movement.

Both education, whatever its limitations, and the communications network of the time made a range of contemporary and historical world events a reality for an increasing number of the poor themselves. The Vietnam revolution, the Chinese revolution, the Black movement and Black poetry, Marxism, the women's movement, the new left, were all part of the cultural mix that represented a world-wide phenomenon. In describing Bombay from its red light districts to its mixed culture and language, the images of Namdev Dhasal, greatest of the early dalit poets and a Panther founder, show a stretch in time, from the crystalised images of India's past to the age of revolutions. They show the consciousness born out of a classic industrialised world juxtaposed with the miseries of village immigrants whose ignorance was symbolised in the mother:

> In the eighteenth century the whole human race was turned upside down,
> but even today you haven't heard of it…
> Mother, your son is not a child.
> He is the son of this age's rebellion,
> he can see clearly the injustice, himself as victim,
> governmental machinery, means of living, power of toil, mines of coal and steel,
> warehouses, factories,
> there: protection, guarantee of food and money,
> my face, lying in the dust, separated from all of this.
> (Dhasal 1992, 60–61)

The early dalit upsurge had a strong Naxalite flavour; dalits identified themselves as modern and proletarian and saw their enemy—Hinduism—as feudal backwardness. Militancy was a crucial aspect of this. As a dalit activist of the Bombay slums recalled the period, "We knew nothing of what was written in the Manifesto. All we knew was that if someone put his hand on your sister—cut it off!" This near nihilist mood and fierce anger distinguished it from early twentieth century movements and made the Dalit Panthers specifically and the whole new dalit movement generally, an aspect of a worldwide 'new left' upsurge. Indeed, it was at this time that the term 'dalit' or downtrodden, the 1930s' and 1940s' Marathi/Hindi translation of this British category of 'Depressed Classes', became widespread: a militant alternative to the Gandhian term 'Harijan' and the colourless governmental 'Scheduled Castes'.

The combining of economic and cultural radicalism was also common to many new left movements of the period. Whereas the traditional Indian left, including the Naxalites, during almost this entire period scarcely spoke of cultural issues or critiqued Hinduism as such, for the young dalit poets, economic and cultural exploitation were interwoven from the beginning. The Manifesto (written under a pronounced Naxalite ideological influence), after condemning Hinduism as feudalism, had really nothing to say about caste issues; the poetry however spoke of caste, of Buddha, of brahmans, of Shambuk and Ekalavya just as it spoke of poverty and the meaninglessness of parliamentary democracy. It ranged over all of Indian history and mythology, claiming a new past as well as laying claim to the future. For the poets it was as important to curse both god and the modern university as it was to expose capitalism—

> One day I cursed that mother-fucker god
> He just laughed shamelessly.
> My neighbour, a born-to-the-pen Brahman, was shocked.
> He looked at me with his castor-oil face...
> I cursed another good hot curse
> The university buildings shuddered and sank waste-deep.

All at once scholars began doing research
into what makes people angry…?
(Meshram 1992, 117)

Their modernism was turned against the caste system, as much as it was turned against economic exploitation:

I stand today at the very end
of the twentieth century.
All around me is in flame…
Taking in one hand the sun, in the other the moon,
I am conscious of my resolve,
the worth of the blood of Ekalavya's broken finger.
(Nimbalkar 1976)

Marxism, as known in India, had separated class and caste oppressions; now the two were sought to be joined. This new project laid the ground for the upsurges of the 1970s and 1980s. The Panthers, in fact, rose and fell like a flash. Their first split came within only two years, rhetorically structured on the lines of 'Buddhism versus Marxism'. Raja Dhale, leader of the Buddhist faction, claimed that his opponent Namdev Dhasal was a tool in the hands of the Marxists. Much of the intense dalit debate at this time took place at a seemingly crude level ('Who is your father: Ambedkar or Marx?') but behind it lay a great fear of being controlled by articulate, sophisticated brahman radicals. And the leftists to a large degree laid themselves open to attack by their ignorance of the rules of the anti-caste discourse (for example, the apparently trivial but symbolically important mistakes of spelling Phule's name as 'Jyotiba' in the brahmanical fashion rather than 'Jotiba' after the village deity continued to be made again and again by upper-caste communists).

Nevertheless, the fragmentation of the Panthers was only an episode in a long upsurge. Not only did dalits continue to organise and fight back but they also provided major themes of revolt to other new assertions of the time. If the proletarianisation of dalit identity was a new universalism, a new claim to being a kind of vanguard it was also an effort to define the entire Indian revolution in terms of the upsurge of the low castes, the theme of 'we are the proletariat' being expressed in numerous poems and constantly in speeches. It was typical, for instance, that the then Panther leader Arun Kamble, speaking of the Mandal Commission and the need for unity between dalits and non-brahmans at a Visham Nirmulan conference in the early 1980s, could argue for a "kunbi-isation" of Marathas (i.e., accepting their identity as toiling peasants rather than as 'village rulers'), and end with the assertion: "We want dalitistan but not dalitistan as a separate country; we are 98.5%, we are the majority, *India shall become dalitistan!*" Dalits were, on such platforms, beginning to define identities and ideologies for other sections of the exploited.

The 1970s saw not only the rise of a new low-caste upsurge, but also the spread of a kind of 'dalit consciousness' to many other movements. This came to signify the uniting of social and economic issues. It was taken up for instance by A. K. Roy, an independent Marxist leader of mine workers and the Jharkhand movement. In a pamphlet called 'The New Dalit Revolution' published in 1980, Roy attacked the entire upper-caste leadership of left movements, attempted to theorise the geographical/social basis of Indian hierarchy in terms of the interaction between a hilly tribal area, a river bank-centred feudal civilisation, and a port city-centred colonial civilisation. Roy called for a fresh "discovery of India" through the participation of intellectuals in movements.

> Whether the Indian bourgeoisie is black or white, big or small has very little bearing on the politics of the country. What really matters are two basic features: caste system with uneven development of history and its interaction with the belated capitalism percolating from the top.... The communists have prepared various blueprints of revolution like National Democratic Revolution, Peoples' Democratic Revolution, New Democratic Revolution, and many other forms using mysterious terms hardly understood or even remembered by their own followers, not to speak of the toiling millions at large, while India needs a simple New Dalit Revolution, a policy of red and green flag combining the struggles for social emancipation with that against economic exploitation to storm the citadel of colonialism in the country.

Roy went on to assert the need for a cultural revolution within the Indian left, insisting that the symbols of the people should not be Rama or Krishna but those of the low-caste masses—often local, tribal and peasant leaders such as Birsa Munda (leader of an adivasi revolt in the nineteenth century), or Veer Narayan Singh (the adivasi chieftain who fought Aurangzeb):

> The culture of the people, struggle of the oppressed like that of Birsa Munda of Chotanagpur and Veer Narayan Singh of Chattisgarh would be highlighted which is now obscured and would be restored to its rightful place above the wars and conspiracies of the feudal kings and colonial rulers which now crowd the pages of history. From Buddha to Lenin it would be a unique journey, a new search for a spirit of emancipating millions, a new religion not only a new party, out to make a new history for mankind without exploitation, subjugation and with justice. (Roy 1980, 4, 10, 18)

Thus, by the late 1970s, as new social movements began to rise throughout the country, taking up the issues of caste, the exploitation of farmers, environmental degradation and its effects on the toiling people, dalits and other 'productive castes' were also beginning to assert themselves. The political thrust was next.

Eleven

The Logic of Dalit Politics

The 'unique journey' that A. K. Roy had called for seemed to be beginning in the 1970s. Numerous youth went to the villages, new activists rose from the masses, social turmoil increased as economic and social pressures mounted, and new voices rose as other low-caste and oppressed sections joined dalits in organising.

Dalit themes were expressed also by tribals, for instance Waharu Sonavane, an adivasi poet-activist coming out of a Marxist-led movement of Bhil agricultural labourers and poor peasants of northern Maharashtra. He was an activist sensitive from the beginning to cultural issues but by the late 1980s these were becoming dominant themes, as he challenged the control of non-tribals in adivasi-based movements. He began to argue that the adivasis who had been fragmented by religious identity and political parties should come together. But while he was willing to include BJP adivasi politicians in this coming together, Waharu clearly identified with the heritage of rakshasas, dismissing Rama as an exploiter and giving a unique adivasi perspective on the entire non-Aryan theme.

A strong alliance between minority of brahmans and a handful of rajas took one after the other adivasi tribes under their control through violence and aggression. They made them into slaves and disarmed toiling peasants paying taxes to rajas, and settled them in villages to enlarge their kingdoms through settled agriculture. Between the sixth century BC, that is the period of Buddha, and the fifth centuries AD a defined caste hierarchy and jajmani system was established. Most free adivasi tribes became toiling castes giving surplus to rajas and brahman–dominated feudal society! This society had the capacity to slowly transform adivasi tribes and absorb them in the hierarchy, but at lower levels. We were those who faced this but remained free.... When the adivasis of that time began to resist the atrocities against them, the Aryans became enraged. Then the Aryans went to the ruler of that time, their raja Shri Ramachandra, with the demand 'protect us from the rakshasas, our herds need open fields.' Rama gave a promise. Under the leadership of Ramchandraji adivasis of that time were slaughtered as rakshasas and crushed.

(Speech to Dalit-Gramin Sahitya Sammelan)[1]

Later, in the 1990s, Waharu joined with other adivasis of Maharashtra, Gujarat, Rajasthan and Madhya Pradesh in organising Adivasi Ekta, a strongly autonomous organisation of tribals.

The 1980s were marked not only by the assertion of dalits and other low castes, but also by the rise of other new social movements, of farmers fighting against their exploitation by the market and state, of women, of tribal and caste Hindu peasants fighting against environmental destruction and displacement. These movements began to identify at least in part—at the beginning—with a critique of Hinduism and to put forward new cultural themes that began to converge with those of the dalit and anti-caste movement. Sometimes they drew consciously on this tradition.

In the new post-1975 women's movement, for example, there was initially a strong rejection by feminists of religion as such, with the underlying theme that 'all religions are patriarchal and oppress women' replacing the pre-independence tendency to take Sita and Savitri as ideals of womanhood. For some time, this religious-cultural critique remained at an abstract level; then in the late 1980s, partly under the impact of the rise of fundamentalism, many women activists began to look for aspects of their own tradition that they

---

[1] Waharu Sonavane, *Presidential Speech*, 5th Adivasi Sahitya Sammelan, Palghar, Maharashtra, 23 December 1990 (translated from Marathi by Gail Omvedt and Bharat Patankar). Originally published in Marathi for the Adivasi Sahitya Sammelan by Sanjay Pethe.

could identify with. For some this meant a clear identification with Hinduism. Madhu Kishwar of the well-known women's magazine *Manushi* attacked only the militaristic and aggressive depiction of Rama by fundamentalists but upheld an ideal Ram. Other feminists looked for what some called 'even more fundamental' religious traditions: at the role played by *devi*s or goddesses in Indian tradition, the co-opting of that role, and ways it might be recovered. In the words of a song by Kamla Bhasin,

> *Every woman in this country is dishonoured, degraded,*
> *With your hand on your heart, say, how can such a country be free?*
> *In this country, they say, there are goddesses without number,*
> *Tell me, have they loosened even a link of our chains?*
> *Have we gained anything of honour from the veil?*
> *Beneath the veil we have remained smothered, beneath the veil we burned...*
> *make the veil into a flag, unfurl it everywhere,*
> *We will bring humanity's rule to this land.*
> *You will not be able to challenge the power of women now!*
> *We are resolved to take on even the form of Kali Mata.*

By late 1980s dalit and other low-caste women, and feminists from south India were also making themselves heard. They tried to recover non-Aryan and anti-brahman traditions, took Sita as a symbol of oppression rather than an ideal, and argued that the Ramayana represented the triumph of patriarchy over matriarchy. Ruth Manorama, a dalit Christian from Bangalore involved in organising slum dwellers, began to speak of the "triply oppressed", focusing on brahmanism as a major factor in women's oppression but not sparing dalit men either. She and others eventually organised the National Federation of Dalit Women. At the 1991 National Women's Studies Conference in Calcutta two minority feminists, Flavia Agnes and Razia Patel, were openly attacking 'Hindu hegemony' in the women's movement.

The environmental movement also saw a similar development, the emergence of culturally radical themes contesting a dominant trend that identified, though more ambiguously than in the colonial period, with a reformist Hinduism. Middle-class environmentalism had been Gandhian in inspiration, mounting a strong ideological attack on industrial civilisation and 'western science and technology' that included a tendency to idealise Indian traditional culture. This even involved some indifference to or even idealisation of caste, with the most important academic study of the 'ecological history of India' giving what was in effect a functionalist justification of caste as a system of ecological adaption (Gadgil and Guha 1992, 91–110). Ecofeminists like Vandana Shiva emphasised the mother-goddess theme in women's writing as the protector of nature and identified it with 'Prakriti' (Shiva 1989). However environmental mass movements based on peasants and other low castes very often used more anti-brahman traditions. Thus a movement for water rights on the river Ganga used the symbol of Ekalavya, with the fishing communities they organised identifying themselves with this tribal hero of the epic. In southern Maharashtra, a strong local farmers' struggle for a peasant-built small dam identified itself with the tradition of Phule and named it the Bali Raja Memorial Dam.

Bali Raja became an important symbol for other mass movements in Maharashtra as well. A group working among other backward castes in the Vidarbha region took it as a major theme of yearly celebrations, and it became also a central symbol for the most powerful mass movement in the state, the Shetkari Sanghatana. Its leader, Sharad Joshi, though himself a brahman, used the symbols of the people to explicate his 'Bharat versus India' contradiction in society between the (mainly urban) exploiting sections and the (mainly rural) exploited. Gandhian models were evoked to stress that village and agriculture-centred development had to be followed rather than one based on state-controlled industry—this was no longer Ram Raj but Bali's kingdom, and the 1989 Nanded conference of the Shetkari Sanghatana took the popular peasant saying but turned it into an affirmative 'troubles and sorrows *will go*, the kingdom of Bali *will come.*' The Karnataka Rayat Sangh, another strong regional farmers' movement, used anti-caste themes from a Lohiaite tradition and tried to make alliances with the dalit movement in Karnataka. On the other hand, leaders of the farmers' movement in the Hindi belt, such as the Jat leader Mahendra Singh Tikait, spoke an anti-brahmanic language but identified with the more orthodox versions of Hinduism popular there.

There was thus an extreme unevenness in the culture of popular movements of the 1980s: a spread of the challenge to orthodox Hindu traditions, but marked at points with what was from the dalit point of view, a compromise with brahmanism on the part of some sections, and at others with a readiness to identify with other religious and cultural fundamentalisms as a counter to brahmanic Hinduism. These counter-fundamentalisms were perhaps strongest in the complex movements arising in the peripheral nationalities. In Punjab, opposition to brahman-bania Delhi rule involved an identification with Sikh religious traditions that at points turned into a strong fundamentalism, including efforts to regulate women's attire and suppression of intellectual inquiry. In Kashmir, Islamic and socialist tendencies were mixed in a guerrilla armed struggle against the centre, and fundamentalist Islamist trends took over when the more secular forces were crushed by the Indian state after 1981. In Assam, much of the movement from 1980 onwards seemed to be dominated by high-caste Hindu students. The more militant armed struggle group, the United Liberation Front of Assam, the ULFA, on the other hand, picked up the theme of north-eastern uniqueness: their Assam, never conquered by Hindus or Muslims, was very largely 'Mongoloid, Tibeto-Mongoloid, and Austric' in contrast to the Aryan-Dravidian mainland, as their petition before the General Assembly of the United Nations put it.

Thus, in many ways the 1980s saw, below the surface of the growth of Hindutva and Congress corruption, complex processes of cultural dialogue. Compared to the colonial period, there was intense interaction between the various forms of opposition to the Indian state, with the left forces also involved in various ways. Yet the period was still marked by ongoing contradictions and a failure to evolve a total liberatory theory.

The logic of dalit politics, it may be argued, involved three major emerging themes:

1. A challenge to the very definition of Hinduism as the majority religion and the core of Indian tradition; an insistence that it was rather a brahmanic Hinduism that represented the hegemony of an elite over that tradition, and that this hegemony had to be overthrown.

2. A spreading of this theme beyond dalits themselves to involve all the sections of the oppressed, exploited and marginalised by the processes of caste exploitation, including adivasis and other backward castes (the former shudras), peasants, women, and oppressed nationalities.
3. A synthesis of a new economic and political direction with the cultural challenge.

For dalit politics to succeed, it may be argued, all of these were necessary. The story of the last three decades has seen an uneven spiralling, a turmoil of assertion. Dalits and other exploited sections have been increasingly asserting themselves—but often at cross purposes, often even in antagonism to one another. At the centre of much of this has been the rise of the Bahujan Samaj Party (BSP), first as an effort to bring all the exploited together, then as a dalit-based party challenging for control in Delhi itself.

The 1980s and 1990s saw the fading of the Congress as the dominant hegemonic party in India, in spite of a temporarily renewed sympathy vote after the assassination of Indira Gandhi and in spite of the 'clean' technologically oriented initial liberalisation represented by her son Rajiv Gandhi. Instead, alternatives were in the air. By the late 1980s it looked for a time as if a new political force could arise from a base in the new social movements to come as an alternative. This was the V. P. Singh-led National Front government, its core the newly formed socialist Janata Dal. All of the new movements, from dalits to farmers to environmentalists, backed it; Datta Samant, the militant unorthodox working class leader, and Sharad Joshi, the most articulate of the new farmers' leader, joined in the campaign.

Yet though V. P. Singh came to power as Prime Minister, his government lasted only a short eleven months. His announcement of the implementation of the Mandal Commission report—caste reservations for 'other backward classes', that is, the former shudra castes—provoked a strong reaction. Agitations broke out among the upper castes, with the attempt at suicide by burning by a young student provoking numerous others, many of whom succeeded. This was followed in October 1990 by a 'rath yatra' campaign of Hindutva forces, now organised under the Bharatiya Janata Party (BJP), led by Lal Krishna Advani, aimed at constructing a Hindu temple in Ayodhya. This time, on 6 December, the mosque at Ayodhya, the 'Babri Masjid', named after Babur, the original Mughal conqueror of India, was demolished, and in the rioting that followed hundreds of people died. Anti-Muslim sentiment surged. Fanatical pro-leaders like Bal Thackeray of Maharashtra's Shiv Sena said openly to *Time* magazine that, "have (Indian Muslims) behaved like the Jews in Nazi Germany? If so, there is nothing wrong if they are treated as Jews were in Nazi Germany... In politics we follow Shivaji. In religion it's Shiva. The third eye is now opening" (*Time* 1993). No one dared arrest him at the time. The V. P. Singh government fell, to be replaced briefly by a caretaker government led by Chandrasekhar, and then the Congress returned to power, following the horrifying assassination of Rajiv Gandhi, on a sympathy vote under the leadership of the old Congress politician, Narasimha Rao.

The BJP thus appeared for a time as a real alternative, a 'different' party. In 2004 and after it made serious challenges for power, it even ruled at the centre for a time, after the 1998 and 2004 elections. Yet by 2008 the appeal of Hindutva seemed to be fading, and after its disastrous defeat in the 2009 elections, the party almost fell apart, with senior leaders such as Jaswant Singh expelled, others resigning or openly defying the party leadership.

Dalits had always mistrusted both parties, and seen Gandhism as only a more seemingly progressive version of Hindutva: after all, massive and horrifying anti-Muslim riots in Gujarat, the centre of Gandhi's influence, seemed to prove that the Hindutva Ram Raj was only a step removed from Gandhi's Ram Raj.

Baburao Bagul, an award-winning writer and one-time Communist party member, had written condemning the hegemony of Hindu themes in the national movement. He argued that in Europe, nationalism and the bourgeois revolution had a progressive content and people had fought religious authority, but in India, nationalism "was turned into a form of ancestor worship". Bagul went on to argue that, since "Hindus are the majority", there was little to hope for from the Indian tradition:

Democratic socialism which is based on liberty, equality and fraternity is the philosophy of the modern age. And this philosophy has no roots in the Indian psyche and mystical value-structure. The literature of the saints has not provided any valuable alternative in the forms of ideals. On the other hand, fascism, yarns-domination, hero-worship, pride, scorn, malice and hatred—all these have solid literary and intellectual support. (Bagul 1992, 283, 288)

A young poet, Vilas Rashinikar, put it equally strongly:

From pitch black tunnels
they gather ashes
floating on jet-black water
and reconstruct the skeletons
of their ancestors,
singing hymns
of their thoughts
worn to shreds.
There is no entry here
for the new sun.
This is the empire
of ancestor-worship,
of blackened cast offs,
of darkness.
(Ibid., 284–85)

Dalit politics, thus, made important strides in the 1980s and 1990s. For most it was indeed a major alternative to the rise of Hindutva. In the 1980s the political alternative resulting from the 'new social movements' proved a failure. But by the end of the decade a new force was coming forward, the Bahujan Samaj Party. This was the latest expression of dalit political force, but its career was to be a strange one.

Twelve

The Rise of the Bahujan Samaj Party

In the late 1970s a riot took place spreading throughout Marathwada after the proposal to rename the university after Dr Ambedkar was put forward; the caste Hindus of Marathwada claimed it denigrated their regional pride and went on a rampage against the dalit Buddhists. In response, the dalits and their progressive friends organised a 'long march' to demand the renaming. This only happened though, years later, as a 'name-expanding' proposal to make it Dr. Ambedkar Marathwada University.

Watching all of this, and scornful of the lack of organising capacity of dalits, was a then-young Chamar from the Punjab employed in the Defense Department in Pune, Kanshi Ram. Kanshi Ram had become interested in 'Ambedkarite' politics following experiences of discrimination at work. He began reading about the movement. He joined the Republican party for some time, but became disgusted with its factionalism and failure to move beyond its dalit Buddhist base. It had become, contrary to Ambedkar's intentions, not simply a 'dalit' party but a party linked to only one dalit caste, the former Mahars. Kanshi Ram was later to say: "I learned much about politics from Maharashtra. From Ambedkar I learned how to do politics. From the Republican Party I learned how not to do politics." The magazine that he had begun to publish described the Long March as "leaderless". To Kanshi Ram, there was no dalit leadership worth the name left in India.

He began his own organising with the founding of the Backward and Minority Community Employees' Federation (BAMCEF). Based on mainly SC government employees, this was designed to provide resources and some activist leadership for a future political movement. He wooed intellectuals, held rallies, held meetings of various caste communities, for he also believed that though the final goal was annihilation of caste, the beginning lay in mobilising through castes. Social enlightenment was part of this; when BAMCEF, Dalit Shoshit Samaj Sangarsh Samiti (DS-4) and later the Bahujan Samaj Party organised in north India and elsewhere, they publicised what Kanshi Ram called the 'four pillars' of social democracy in India—Ambedkar, Phule, Shahu Maharaj of Kolhapur, and Periyar.

Then he founded DS-4 and it fought the first elections in the early 1980s. This was later to be transformed into the Bahujan Samaj Party, founded in 1984. Its gains at first were modest; its policy was to put up candidates everywhere, even if they were to lose their deposit. The idea was also to accumulate enough votes at the national level to claim to be a 'national' party. When this happened, the BSP claimed as its symbol the elephant, previously the symbol of the Republican Party whose base was mainly in Maharashtra—a symbol which had followed Ambedkar's choice of the name, from the US based Republican party considered to be the party of Lincoln and hence of the ending of slavery.

Nationally few seats were won, but by the 1999 elections it won 13 parliamentary seats and in 2009 it won 17. Its share of votes in 2009, almost 7 per cent, made it the third largest party in India, replacing the disaster-caught Left parties.

Uttar Pradesh remained its strongest base. Here Kanshi Ram brought in a young dalit woman, Mayawati, as his chief lieutenant, in effect giving her control of the party. Here the BSP had a natural base in the Chamar community, the largest of the Scheduled Castes who made up almost 20 per cent of the population. In 1993 the BSP won the assembly elections in Uttar Pradesh in alliance with the Socialist Party. It was around this point, apparently, that Mayawati, who became the Chief Minister, grabbed control of the party. By now the BSP was publicising not only the 'four pillars' but also women leaders such as Zhalkaribai, a fighter from the OBCs during the 1857 war.

Kanshi Ram went south, moving into Andhra, Goa, Maharashtra, winning new recruits from the Left in the flush of enthusiasm of the UP victory. In Maharashtra, he said he was looking for the "Mulayam"—a *bahujan* leader to take charge of the party. With Naganath Naikaudi, a Maratha and an old freedom fighter, he seemed to have found his man. The issue they took up was also very 'Maratha'-oriented: renaming Pune University after Shahu Maharaj, the former Maharaja of Kolhapur, beloved among dalits as well as non-Brahmans generally for (among other things) initiating the reservation policy—but anathema to the brahmans who took Pune as their cultural centre. Kanshi Ram was, in other words, making the BSP truly 'bahujan'[1] but with dalit leadership. One result was to provoke Prakash Ambedkar, leading one of the factions of the Republican party, to form a 'Bahujan Mahasangh' as an alliance; this had some success in parts of Vidarbha.

Progress of BSP in National Parliamentary Elections

Year	Cong	BJP	BSP
1952	45.00	03.10	
1957	47.80	05.90	
1962	44.70	06.40	
1967	40.80	09.40	
1971	43.70	07.40	
1977	34.50	–	
1980	42.70	–	
1984	48.10	07.40	
1989	39.50	11.50	
1991	36.50	20.10	
1996	28.80	20.29	3.64
1998	25.72	25.38	4.66
1999	28.3	23.75	4.16
2004	26.44	22.16	
2009	29.02	19.12	6.98

---

[1] 'Bahujan' literally means 'majority people' and was used by the party to stress the unity of dalits, former shudras, adivasis and religious minorities.

But the promised expansion did not take place. Tensions grew between Mayawati's BSP and Mulayam Singh's Samajwadi Party (SP), and eventually support was withdrawn. Instead of possibly resigning and fighting for BSP politics, Mayawati decided to remain as Chief Minister with the support of the BJP. This was to be consistent with her politics in the next few years. In control of the party, she consistently refused an alliance with the Congress, flirting instead with the BJP, even campaigning once for Narendra Modi in Gujarat after the pogrom against Muslims in 2002 had disgraced him.

Then, with the 2007 assembly elections coming in UP, Mayawati made a major shift in the party policy. She changed the policy of opposing brahmans and instead began to woo them. 'Bahujan samaj' was in the process of becoming 'sarva samaj'—the whole society. Part of this was a resultant of the unique electoral arithmetic of UP—12 per cent brahmans, 12 per cent other 'upper' castes, 20 per cent dalits. With the largest section of OBCs—the Yadavas under Mulayam Singh—resolutely aligned against her, the brahman alliance seemed to make sense. But she was not asking brahmans to change—in the way that the Black movement earlier in the US had demanded that whites give up their racism to join the movement. She was not asking them to join a movement, but was wooing them for electoral support. A new slogan began to be heard: "Haathi naahi, Ganesh hai—Brahma, Vishnu Mahesh hai."

Many dalits began to feel a sense of betrayal. But Mayawati's success—for she had a major win at the elections, the BSP getting enough seats so that she could form the government without support from any other party—silenced most of them. Though she was sidelining many of the old, loyal BSP cadre, she was clearly in command of a winning party—and that made all the difference. Since Kanshi Ram had died, she had no rivals for hegemony.

Mayawati was fast becoming the 'bad girl' of Indian politics—in contrast to Sonia Gandhi, the 'good girl' now firmly in control of the Congress acting the perfect widow, renouncing power herself and preparing the way for her son Rahul as she supported Manmohan Singh for the position of Prime Minister. Where Sonia wore saris, usually draped over her head, speaking better and better

Hindi as she learned her way, Mayawati, kept her hair short, wore white Punjabi-style dresses, celebrated her birthdays throwing huge parties where she flashed her diamonds; in a sense, she was breaking all the rules. For her dalit followers however, it hardly mattered: she was winning for them.

Then came the 2009 parliamentary elections. As the parties geared up, there appeared to be no 'winning wave'. Congress was discredited and BJP factionalised between its hard-core Hindutva group and the more sophisticated leaders who wanted to fashion an ideology mainly of development because it appeared that Hindutva was no longer a winning strategy for them. There were dozens of regional parties, and more were getting formed all the time, often based on OBCs proclaiming a regional identity. In Bihar, Nitish Kumar had sidelined Lalu Prasad Yadav and was promoting a developmental agenda. In Maharashtra, Sharad Pawar's National Congress Party was renewing its hopes for a drive for the prime ministership. Fronts were getting formed right and left, but none— outside of Congress, which continued to push for Manmohan Singh—could agree on leadership. Mayawati announced her own aspirations, joined a 'third front' with the Left but refused to take part in any 'Common Minimum Programme' or promote a leader. She was aiming on her own, and trying to take her brahman alliance agenda to the national level.

She ran a flashy campaign, dashing around the country, nearly singlehandedly representing the BSP, talking of "social transformation". BSP cadres throughout the country geared up, dalits excitedly began to talk of political power. She began to get national and international publicity being one of the only non-Congress, non-BJP leaders to have done so. Mayawati was too colourful to be ignored. Some of the publicity was very cynical, such as *Newsweek*'s 'India's Anti-Obama' which strikingly argued in American-style against what they saw as hard-class politics. But it was publicity, and partly because of the elections, that the issue of caste in India began to get worldwide publicity.

Yet when the votes were counted, it was clear that the BSP had failed. Among other things, dalits in UP itself were frustrated with Mayawati: according to reporter Shivam Vij, they were unhappy that she had taken them for granted and, not ready to vote against her, stayed away from the polls.

This means for sure that had the Dalit voter not decided to make her/his resentment apparent, the BSP could well have got 35+ seats, and perhaps halted the Congress and become a key coalition partner.

But UP's Dalits knew she was flying too far and fast. They didn't want to lose her to Delhi.[2]

The elections ended with Congress seemingly solidly in power, an outcome celebrated by most intellectuals and journalists, who in the words of Pratap Bhanu Mehta in *Indian Express*, "celebrate the defeat of opportunism, obfuscation and obscurantism ... the era of votebank politics as we have known it is over." By this, of course, he meant politics focusing on issues of caste and regional-linguistic identities. The caste-based parties, and the local parties seemed to have been defeated.

Yet the Congress victory was not nearly so solid in terms of percentages as in terms of seats; and dalits and aspiring 'backward castes' remained in turmoil. Mayawati had disappointed them; the BSP had come close to power at the centre itself, though very often it seemed as if dalit empowerment was taking place at the cost of the loss of the dalit visions.

---

[2] Shivam Vij, http://kafila.org/2009/05/21/ups-dalits-remind-mayawati-democracy-is-a-beautiful-thing/.

Conclusion

Sita's Curse, Shambuk's Silence

There is an overwhelming consensus among scholars and journalists (not to speak of a large section of common people) that India is a nation of Hindus (or a Hindu majority nation), and that the main fight is between communalists and secularists over its definition. Yet, this consensus is based on surprisingly thin logic. Take, for instance, this passage from an *Economist* article on 'The Hindu Upsurge':

> What is a Hindu? The answer is surprisingly complex. Thousands of years ago, Aryans from Central Asia migrated to the Indian subcontinent, conquering the local tribes. The holy books of the Aryans, the Vedas, were a mixture of philosophy, prayers and stories about their many gods. As the Aryans mingled with the original inhabitants, many local beliefs and further gods joined the Vedic ones. This loose conglomeration of deities and beliefs came to be called Hinduism. The word originally referred to people living around the Indus river. It has always denoted a society rather than a faith, let alone a church.... (*Economist* 1993, 21)

This is an apparently objective account; but it does not mention that the subcontinent contained not simply 'tribes' but also a civilisation, and takes 'Aryan' as the foundation element to which other religious themes are added. Yet, in repeating for us the theme that 'Hindus' represent both a people and a set of beliefs (religion), it pinpoints a very clear dilemma. If Hinduism is a religion, then it cannot denote simply those living in the subcontinent, and as a religion (linked to brahmanism, a belief in the authority of the Vedas, and caste) it is not the original or national religion of the subcontinent. Many others (Buddhism, Jainism) can well claim to be older and still other religious definitions (Sikhism, Veerasaivism, tribal traditions) can legitimately claim to be outside the Hindu consensus. Hinduism, defined as a religion, cannot so easily claim majority status.

On the other hand, if Hinduism denotes a society—or a people living in a particular territory—then it can well claim cultural traditions reaching back to Mohenjo-daro and beyond, as well as encompass the diversity of races, ethnic groups and cultural particularities ranging from Kashmir to Kanyakumari, the north-east to the Rajasthan desert and beyond. But by this definition, which would include in the people all those incursions from outside the subcontinent as well (beginning with the Aryans and Dravidians themselves), there is no ground to exclude Indian Muslims and Indian Christians, to make any conditionalities upon their acceptance, or to take Rama, Krishna or any of the particular localised deities as definatory of a supposed national consensus. There is certainly no historical or logical ground to prioritise a Vedic tradition. *This type of Hindu identity (which some would call Sindhu-Hindu on the grounds that Sindhu is after all the original pronunciation)* (Patankar 1993) *has clear equalitarian and anti-brahmanic connotations.*

In other words, the construction of Hinduism as achieved by the Hindu-nationalists and accepted in various forms by many supposed secularists as well, rests on a trick: conflating the two contradictory definitions of a broad, territorial, pluralistic, historical identity with a religious culture that continues to give dominance to an Aryan/Vedic/Sanskritic/brahmanic core.

The article in the *Economist* goes on to say that the problem is not a Hindu-Muslim one but "an argument between secular and communal Hindus over the treatment of Muslims." But the issue is different and far deeper than this. The argument—the great cultural debate, the class/caste struggle—is over 'what is Hindu' and 'what is Indian', and it is, in the end, between the upholders of a brahmanic, patriarchal tradition and the exploited low-caste masses.

This is where the Aryan issue becomes significant. Phule had propounded the theory of the Aryan invasion as the source of oppression; dalit radicals of the 1920s took it to its extreme; Ambedkar denied it. The crude version of this dalit anti-Aryanism, as scholars are quick to point out, is fallacious as well as a form of inverted racism: there is no real evidence that the Aryans were responsible for destroying the Indus valley civilisation, and tracing the caste system solely to events of conquest is inadequate. Yet the imagery survives and for good reasons. The continual privileging of an Aryan identity and a Vedic-Upanishadic-Sanskritic core by almost all upper-caste definers of Indian tradition, the pride in being 'white' in opposition to 'black', the continual assumptions of northern superiority, the continual if always veiled forms of upper-caste arrogance: all of these make it almost inevitable that the angry dalit-shudra masses will throw back the weapon of racial and ethnic identity and ask again, "Who was the first invader? Who was the first outsider?"

The issue of brahmanism is as central as that of Aryanism. The attack on brahmanism can be theoretically differentiated from a rejection of the brahmans, yet one slides easily into another form of discourse on caste, feeding the already powerful fears of losing caste-linked privileges and power in a way that can become explosive—as the wave of rioting and suicide following the announced implementation of the Mandal Commission report indicated. It is easy enough to point out that casteist prejudices and exclusiveness are pervasive at all levels of the hierarchy, that anti-brahmanism itself often takes racist forms, that merely attacking one section will not by itself provide an alternative for a humane society. Yet brahmanism seems clearly implicated. Militant anti-caste leaders such as Phule and Ambedkar, both of who had brahman colleagues, were quite rigorous about the conditions of their acceptance: for Phule, the Arya-bhats could be welcomed as long as they 'threw away their bogus scriptures'; for Ambedkar, Hinduism could be saved if all the 'Smrutis and Shastras' were given up.

This has been the simple demand of the anti-caste movement against the dominant elite. However, it has not happened; rather the issue has been evaded, either on secular grounds which claim that after all the solution must be political or economic (because it is the political use of religion which is producing the virus, or it is economic crisis which makes people turn in desperation to solutions of identity); or on reformist Hindu grounds which claim that the texts can be reinterpreted sufficiently to challenge the claims of the brahmans and shankaracharyas to represent them. Despite the continual simmering of the dalit, minority, anti-caste challenge from below, the face of India remains a (brahmanic) Hindu one.

This leads many to despair and nihilism. For several militant dalits, as Bagul's essay shows, there is no hope in tradition; the Hindu majority (defined by brahmanism and Rama) is a solid one; the entire literature and mythology is pervaded with brahmanism. Shudras and ati-shudras had been completely excluded from the literature, whether of the high or low tradition, and where they existed they illustrated only the repressiveness of the system and its ability to prevent or co-opt revolts against it. Bagul argues:

> The enemy had, of course, pervaded Indianness in its entirety; in traditions and customs, in the structure and system, in the books, words and minds....The caste system pervaded the life of the entire society. The intelligentsia were committed to religion.... Hindu writers, therefore, find it difficult to cope with the Ambedkarite hero who is a rebel with a scientific and rationalist attitude; on the other hand, heroes like Kama and Ekalavya are consistent with the cultural and mythical value-structure they have internalised... (They) are reconciled to the varna system; they are courageous, but because they have been denied the place they deserve in the system, they view life only in terms of suffering; these heroes ... become simply toys in the hands of fate. (Bagul 1992, 123–26)

Thus, Kama, Vidura, Ekalavya (the low-caste heroes in the puranas) all in their different ways actually served the brahmanical and feudal system despite their victimisation by it, and Shambuk, the shudra boy killed for the 'sin' of attempting to follow brahmanical yoga, is silent in the face of the forces ranged against him, much as in a film on atrocities against tribals (*Aakrosh*), the tribal male hero is silent except for a cry of protest. Against this, the dalits could only protest: while Ekalavya for example, was to be important for them as an illustration of what varnashrama dharma meant, they wanted him to do what the myths did not reveal him doing—revolt:

> *If you had kept your thumb*
> *History would have happened*
> *somehow differently.*
> *But... you gave your thumb*
> *and history also*
> *became theirs.*
> *Ekalavya,*
> *since that day they*
> *have not even given you a glance.*
> *Forgive me, Ekalavya, I won't be fooled now*
> *by their sweet words.*
> *My thumb*
> *will never be broken.*
> (Hingonekar 1989)

In the face of this apparently overwhelming oppressiveness of tradition, dalit radicals could only respond with a total negation:

> *You who have made the mistake of being born in this country*
> *must now rectify it: either leave the country, or make war!*
> (Bagul 1992, 70)

But is Indian tradition totally oppressive? Is it necessary for either dalit or upper caste progressives who aspire to equality and liberation to reject Indian culture and identity totally? The whole point of the cultural critique from Jotiba Phule and Tarabai Shinde through Ambedkar, Periyar and others was to the contrary: their interpretations of Indian history and tradition rested not only on the negative exposure of caste hierarchy and domination but also on attempts to explore the rebellions and occasional triumphs of the low castes. And conversely, the problem with Nehruvian secularism in fighting a Hindu fundamentalism was not that it was secular and equalitarian, not that it asserted universal values of freedom and equality, but that in order to justify these it simply adopted without criticism the hegemonic, brahmanic interpretation of the tradition. Freedom and equality can in fact find their roots in tradition if that tradition is critically understood.

This requires a process of reinterpretation, because the voice of low castes, women, tribals, non-Aryans, etc. in myths was from the beginning filtered through the interpretations of their masters and conquerors. Shambuk was not silent, he was silenced; his voice was not recorded. Ekalavya may well have fought, but his fight has been erased from myths. In many cases though, the resistance was at least partially recorded, sometimes in the written versions of the legends and sometimes in folk versions that had to be recovered, searched out, and brought to a position of hegemony. These may seem obvious points, something that any social scientist and historian interpreting popular mythology knows: the document itself has been produced in a social process. It should not be necessary in these days of deconstructionism and post-modernism to point this out. But it has become necessary to repeat such points because even the academic interpretations of Indian culture, the ones most influenced by supposedly sophisticated methodologies, have very often taken the high-caste versions of the myths for granted, as texts which are taken to be the unexamined basis for theorising.

Here the feminists attempting to unravel the complexities of Hindu patriarchal co-option have major contributions to offer the dalit contestation of Hinduism. The most interesting example of a suppressed, partly voiceless, seemingly co-opted heroine is Sita, the apparent paradigm of self-sacrificial devotion to a husband. In recent years she has been taken more often as the symbol of women's victimisation. But there is much more to Sita than this, as even a reading of Valmiki's version of the Ramayana makes clear. Thus, we find her, for example, rebuking Rama in the name of the rakshasas:

> You are alarmingly close to that sinful state to which the ignorant are prone ... that is, killing a creature who has not committed any offence.... O hero, my prayer is that when armed with the bow, you are engaged in waging war against the rakshasas, who have

this forest for their home, you may never allow yourself to slay indiscriminately those who are not to blame. (Kishwar 1993)

But in reply, Rama makes it clear that his killing of the rakshasas, including the rakshasa queen Tataka, is out of a vow made to the brahmans of the Dandakaranya forest, and thus as part of a protection of caste hierarchy.

Even more important, beyond the Valmiki Ramayana, and its even more patriarchal successors (such as the Tulsidas Ramayana, which brought in the theme of the *lakshman rekha*) we find in Sita inclinations to rebel. Some traditions depict her love for Ravana (indicating perhaps that this may be a subterranean theme of even the orthodox version in which she is only suspected). There is a strong peasant-based tradition of Sita that emphasises her rejection of Rama after she has been sent away, her anger at the injustices done to her. In a folk poem of Uttar Pradesh for instance, Sita refuses to go back even when Laxman has been sent to bring her, and instead raises her sons on her own and gives them her father's name, in a half-way return to matriliny. The Thai version of the Ramayana, similarly, ends with Sita refusing to go back until the gods themselves intervene to restore family propriety (see Cadet 1970, 242).

One of the most interesting variations of the image of Sita comes from Maharashtra, the Sita of Raveri, and has been picked up by the Shetkari Sanghatana. Raveri is a small village in Yeotmal district where Sanghatna activists, in the process of a campaign to get peasants to put land in the names of the women of their family had come across an old, nearly abandoned Sita temple. "Rakshasas built it," say the villagers, and in fact the image is that of the typical village *devi*. In the story of Raveri, Sita after being forced to leave Ayodhya, wanders and settles in Raveri and because she has two small babies and cannot work, goes from house to house begging for flour. When the villagers refuse to give it (on the grounds that such an abandoned women must be a 'bad woman') she curses that the village will not be able to grow wheat. Sure enough, say the villagers, they could not, until a few years back when hybrid varieties came in. Now, however, they are putting land in the name of women as a way of redressing the sins of their ancestors! There is also a Hanuman temple in the village with a more recently found 'fallen Hanuman'—shot down by Sita's sons, people say, when he came to fetch her back.

Such versions where Sita is not simply a symbol of oppression but linked with rakshasas and identified with agriculture (but not 'green revolution' agriculture), illustrates the real depth of all the counter depictions of the Ramayana: not as the story of Rama's triumph and the ideal family, but a story of his conquest over Dravidian and tribal native inhabitants, of the triumph of patriarchy over matriarchy, of the suppression of women connected with the establishment of a stable agricultural society (Sita is after all *bhumikanya* Sita, found below a furrow). It is ultimately a story which has many renditions in a long era of class/caste/gender struggle, of a conquest over a long time span, but also of the resistance and uniting of the conquered, a reversal, a forecasting of the liberation of peasants, dalits, women, and tribals.

The themes of caste domination, exploitation, and patriarchy come together, and Shambuk, Sita, Tataka, and Ravana are united in their victimisation by the brahmanic Hindu system, and their rebellion against it. It is no longer possible to raise the image of Rama without confronting the totality of the story, and the debate is no longer being carried on simply by an upper-caste educated elite. The themes of victimisation and rebellion are themes that remain linked with the material life of the people, of peasants, women, dalits and tribals, and for that reason, threaten to burst forward even when the Hindutva attempt to hegemonise and crystallise the Ramayana as a symbol of Hindu orthodoxy seems closest to success. Reinterpretations and debates concerning the traditions of Gandhi and Nehru, as well as those of Ambedkar, Phule and Periyar will go on, but so different is the situation from the colonial period that Ram raj is no longer a viable ideal in India today any more than Nehruvian socialism.

Desperate beatings on the drums of an imagined upper-caste past will produce no longlasting victories. The evocation of the people's past will continue to have a role in the formulation of a new society, in which the major dalit theme remains that of confidence and aspiration, symbolised by numerous poems evoking a new sun, by the powerful call of the dalit balladeer Waman Kardak:

Chase away the army of darkness
search the sky, the moon, the stars
the light is in you
the light is in you
be tomorrow's sun.
(Kaidak 1992, 95)

"Sun" is *ravi* in Indian languages; and the ancient dream of 'Begumpura', the city without sorrow, imagined by the bhakti poet Ravidas, imagined again under different names by Tukaram, Kabir, Phule in his "kingdom of Bali" and even in Ambedkar's dream of an "enlightened" India or *prabuddha Bharat* remains as an essence of the 'dalit vision'. The vision remains still far away, but, like the theme of empowerment represented in somewhat distorted form by today's Bahujan Samaj Party, it is very much on the agenda of the new Indian uprising.

Bibliography

Ambedkar, B. R. 1979. 'Annihilation of Caste'. In *Dr. Babasaheb Ambedkar: Writings and Speeches, Volume 1.* Bombay: Government of Maharashtra.

———. 1979. 'Federation or Freedom'. In *Dr. Babasaheb Ambedkar: Writings and Speeches, Volume 1.* Bombay: Government of Maharashtra.

———. 1987. 'Revolution and Counter-Revolution in Ancient India'. *Dr. Babasaheb Ambedkar: Writings and Speeches, Volume 3.* Bombay: Government of Maharashtra.

Bagul, Baburao. 1992a. 'You Who Have Made the Mistake'. Translated by Vilas Sarang. In *Poisoned Bread: Translations from Modern Marathi Dalit Literature*, ed. Arjun Dangle. New Delhi: Orient Longman.

———. 1992b. 'Dalit Literature is but Human Literature'. In *Poisoned Bread: Translations from Modern Marathi Dalit Literature*, ed. Arjun Dangle. New Delhi: Orient Longman.

Banerjee, Sumanta. 1989. 'Women's Popular Culture in Nineteenth Century Bengal'. In *Recasting Women: Essays in Colonial History*, ed. Kumkum Sangari and Sudesh Vaid. Delhi: Kali for Women Press.

Bhagwat, M. E. 1980. 'Vidarbhatil Dalit Vicharanci Netrutva'. In *Political Ideas and Leadership in Vidarbha*, ed. P. L. Joshi. Nagpur: Department of Political Science, Nagpur University.

Bhave, Sadashiv. 1988. 'Bhakti in Modern Marathi Poetry'. In *The Experience of Hinduism*, ed. Eleanor Zelliot and Maxine Berntsen. Albany, New York: State University of New York Press.

Diehl, Anita. 1977. *Periyar E. V. Ramaswami.* Bombay: B. I. Publications.

Cadet, J. M. 1970. *Ramakien: The Stone Rubbings of the Thai Epic.* Bangkok: Kodansha International.

Census of India, 1931, Volume XXIII, Hyderabad State; Part I: Report. 1933. Hyderabad–Deccan: Government Central Press.

Chakravarti, Uma. 1998. *Gender, Class and Nation: Ramabai and the Critique of Brahmanical Patriarchy.* New Delhi: Kali for Women.

———. 1983. 'The Development of the Sita Myth: A Case Study'. *Samya Shakti*, vol. I, no. 1, July.

———. 1993. 'Conceptualising Brahmanical Patriarchy in Early India: Gender, Class and State'. *Economic and Political Weekly*, 3 April.

———. 1981. 'The Sita Who Refused the Fire Ordeal'. *Manushi*, No. 8.

'A summary of the Proceedings'. 1991. In *Jotiba Phule: An Incomplete Renaissance, Seminar Papers.* Surat: Centre for Social Studies.

Chatterjee, Partha. 1989. 'The Nationalist Resolution of the Women's Question'. In *Recasting Women: Essays in Colonial History*, ed. Kumkum Sangari and Sudesh Vaid. Delhi: Kali for Women Press.

Collected Works of Mahatma Jotirao Phule, Volume II, Selections translated by P. G. Patil. 1991. Bombay: Government of Maharashtra.

Cowell, E. B. ed. and trans. 1895. *The Jataka or Stories of the Buddha's former births*, vol. 5. Originally published Cambridge: Cambridge University Press, 1895. Reprinted Delhi: Motilal Banarasidass.

———. ed. 1907. *The Jataka or Stories of the Buddha's former births*, vol. 6, trans. E. B. Cowell and W. H. D. Rouse. Cambridge: Cambridge University Press.

Dhasal, Namdev. 1992. 'So That my Mother May be Convinced', trans. Jayant Karve, Vidyut Bhagwat, and Eleanor Zelliot. In *An Anthology of Dalit Literature*, ed. Mulk Raj Anand and Eleanor Zelliot. New Delhi: Gyan Publishing House.

Economist. 1993. 6 February.

Everett, Jana. 1981. *Women and Social Change in India.* New Delhi: Heritage.

Gadgil, Madhav, and Ramchandra Guha. 1992. *This Fissured Land: An Ecological History of India.* New Delhi: Oxford University Press.

Gautam, M. G. 1976. '"The Untouchables" Movement in Andhra Pradesh'. *Andhra Pradesh State Harijan Souvenir.* Hyderabad; Government Press.

Geetha, V. and S. V. Rajadurai. 1993. 'NeoBrahmanism: An Intentional Fallacy?'. *Economic and Political Weekly*, 16–23 January.

Guna. 1984. *Asiatic Mode: A Soda-Cultural Perspective*. Delhi: Bookwell Publications.

Hawley, John Straughton and Mark Juergensmeier. 1988. *Songs of the Saints of India*. New York: Oxford University Press.

Hingonekar, Shashikant. 'Ekalavya'. *Asmitadarsh*, April/May/June 1989; translated by Gail Omvedt and Bharat Patankar.

Hunger 1992: Second Annual Report on the State of World Hunger. 1992. Washington, D. C.: Bread for the World Institute.

IBRD, *The World Development Report, 1992*. 1992. New Delhi: World Bank.

Irschick, Eugene. 1969. *Politics and Social Conflict in South India*. Berkeley: University of California Press.

——. 1986. *Tamil Revivalism in the 1930s*. Madras: Cre-A.

Iyer, Raghavan. ed. 1986. *The Moral and Political Writings of Mahatma Gandhi, Volume I*. Oxford: Clarendon Press.

Jeurgensmeier, Mark. 1982. *Religion as Social Vision: The Movement against Untouchabilility in 20th Century Punjab*. Berkeley: University of California Press.

Joshi, Barbara. 1984. *Untouchable! Voices of Dalit Liberation*. London: Zed Books.

Kabir. 1997. *Kabir Bijak*. Commentary by Abhilash Das, trans. Prem Prakash. Allahabad: Parakh Prakashak Kabir Sansthan.

Kaidak, Waman. 1992. 'The Darkness within Me'. In *An Anthology of Dalit Literature*, ed. Mulk Raj Anand and Eleanor Zelliot. New Delhi: Gyan Publishing House.

Kailasapathy, K. 1987. 'The Writings of the Tamil Siddhas'. In *The Sants: Studies in a Devotional Tradition of India*, ed. Karine Schomer and W. H. McLeod. Delhi: Motilal Banarsidass.

Khare, R. S. 1984. *The Untouchable as Himself: Ideology, Identity and Pragmatism Among the Lucknow Chamars*. London: Cambridge University Press.

Kishwar, Madhu. 1993. *Times of India*, 28 January.

Kosambi, Meera. 1992. 'Indian Response to Christianity, Church and Colonialism: Case of Pandita Ramabai'. *Economic and Political Weekly*, 24–31 October.

Kumar, Kapil. 1989. 'Rural Women in Oudh, 1917–1947'. In *Recasting Women: Essays in Colonial History*, ed. Kumkum Sangari and Sudesh Vaid. Delhi: Kali for Women Press.

Lal, Deepak. 1988. *The Hindu Equilibrium, I: Cultural Stability and Economic Stagnation, India c.1500 BC–AD 1980*. London: Oxford University Press.

Lynch, Owen. 1969. *The Politics of Untouchability*. New York: Columbia University Press.

Meshram, Keshav. 1992. Untitled poem. In *An Anthology of Dalit Literature*, ed. Mulk Raj Anand and Eleanor Zelliot. New Delhi: Gyan Publishing House.

Moore, R. J. 1990. 'Jinnah and the Pakistan Demand'. In *India, Rebellion to Republic*, ed. Robin Jeffrey et al. New Delhi: Sterling Publishers Pvt. Ltd.

Murugesan, K. and C. Subramanyam. 1975. *Singaravelu, First Communist in South India*. New Delhi: Peoples' Publishing House.

Namboodiripad, E. M. S. 1986. *A History of the Indian Freedom Movement*. Trivandrum: Social Scientist Press.

Namdev. 1999. *Sant Namdevance Abhanggaatha*. Satara: Rashtriya Samiti.

Nehru, Jawaharlal. 1941. *Towards Freedom: The Autobiography of Jawaharlal Nehru*. New York: John Day Co.

———. *The Discovery of India*. 1982. New Delhi: Oxford University Press.

Nimbalkar, Waman. 1976. 'Just Poem', trans. Graham Smith. *Vagartha*, 12 January.

O'Hanlon, Rosalind. 1988. *Caste, Conflict and Ideology; Mahatma Jotiba Phule and Low-Caste Social Protest in Nineteenth Century Western India*. Cambridge: Cambridge University Press.

Omvedt, Gail. 1994. *Dalits and the Democratic Revolution: Dr. Ambedkar and the Dalit Movement in Colonial India*. New Delhi: Sage.

Pandey, Gyanendra. 1991. 'Hindus and Others: The Militant Hindu Construction'. *Economic and Political Weekly*, 28 December.

———. 1990. *The Construction of Communalism in Colonial North India*. Delhi: Oxford University Press.

Patankar, Bharat. 1993. *Hindu ka Sindhu*. Pune: Sugawa Prakashan, 1993. A shortened English version, Hindu or Sindhu'. *Frontier*, 27 February.

Phukon, Girin. 1986. 'Ethnic Nationalism in North-East India: A Brief Overview of its Legacy'. In Deka, *North-East Quarterly*, vol. 2, no. 3.

Phule, Jotiba. 1990. *Samagra Wanghmay*. Bombay: Government of Maharashtra.

Ramabai, Pandita. 1982. *The High-Caste Hindu Woman*. Originally published 1887. Reprinted Bombay: Government of Maharashtra.

Ramanujan, A. K. trans. 1973. *Speaking of Siva*. New Delhi: Penguin.

Ramteke, Kamalsingh Baliram. 1941. Untitled poem. *Janata*, 21 June.

——. Untitled poem. 1938. *Janata*, 15 January.

Roy, A. K. 1980. *The New Dalit Revolution*.

Roy, Asim. 1991. 'The High Politics of India's Partition: The Revisionist Perspective (Review Articles)'. *Modern Asian Studies*, vol. 24, no. 2, May.

Sarkar, Sumit. 1983. *Modern India, 1885–1947*. Delhi: Macmillan India Ltd.

Schouten, J. P. 1995. *Revolution of the Mystics: On the Social Aspects of Virasaivism*. Delhi: Motilal Banarsidass.

Shinde, Tarabai. 1992. *Stri-Purush Tulna*. Nagpur: Asoka Prakashan.

Shiva, Vandana. 1989. *Staying Alive: Women and Ecology in India*. New Delhi: Kali for Women Press.

Shivaiah, M. 1993. 'Behind Hindu Growth Rate'. *Economic and Political Weekly*, 3 April.

The Challenge to the South: Report of the South Commission. New Delhi: Oxford University Press, 1992.

Time. 1993. 25 January.

Tukaram. 1973. *Shri Tukarambavancya Abhangaci Gatha*. Marathi collection of Tukaram's Abhangs. Mumbai: Shaskiya Madhyavati Mudranalay.

Upreti, G. B. 1997. The Early Buddhist World Outlook in Historical Perspective, New Delhi: Manohar.

Vithal, B. P. R. 1993. 'Roots of Hindu Fundamentalism'. *Economic and Political Weekly*, 20–27 February.

Yechury, Sitaram. 1993. 'What is Hindu Rashtra? An Exposure of Golwalkar's Fascist Ideology and the Saffron Brigade's Practice'. *Frontline*, 12 March.

Recommended Readings

Aloysius, G. 1997. *Nationalism without a Nation in India.* **New Delhi: Oxford University Press.**
Aloysius, a Christian OBC from Tamil Nadu, after working for over a decade as an activist in Jharkhand, returned to Delhi and took up his education. This is his M.Phil dissertation, a hard-hitting critique of all the well-known nationalist leaders and a survey of the anti-caste movements of the colonial period.

Ambedkar, B. R. 2005. *Annihilation of Caste.* **New Delhi: Critical Quest Publications.**
This is a reprint of a 1936 essay; Ambedkar had been asked to give a lecture in the Punjab on the subject, but the Jat-Pat Todak Mandal which invited him refused to publish it as it was, objecting to some of his stronger critiques. Ambedkar published it on his own, along with a reply by Gandhi and his response. This is a powerful critique of Hinduism.

——. 2006. *The Philosophy of Hinduism.* **New Delhi: Critical Quest Publications.**
This elucidates what a philosophy should do, how different philosophies and religions have developed according to stages of society, and from the basis of modernism (where the individual not the group is the centre of morality) critiques Hinduism with abundant quotes from Manu and others.

Chakravarti, Uma. 1998. *Rewriting History: The Life and Times of Pandita Ramabai.* **New Delhi: Kali for Women.**
An engrossing study not only of Ramabai (and here it gives almost the definitive source) but also of her age, including Phule, Ranade, the Peshwas and others. Uma Chakravarti is a well-known scholar of ancient India, who was first to use the concept of 'brahmanical patriarchy'.

Geetha, V. and S. V. Rajadurai. 1998. *Towards a Non-Brahmin Millennium: From Iyothee Thass to Periyar.* **Calcutta: Samya.**
A good analysis of the anti-caste movement in Tamil Nadu, beginning with the first reviver of Buddhism in India, the dalit Iyothee Thass. Geetha and Rajadurai also include the issues of how the movement handled feminism.

Hawley, John Straughton and Mark Juergensmeier. 1988. *Songs of the Saints of India.* **New York: Oxford University Press.**
A good survey, with translations, of some of the most important *sant*s (includes Ravidas, Kabir, Tulsidas, Surdas), by two American scholars. It also gives descriptions of the current state of the movements around these icons.

Hess, Linda and Shukhdev Singh. trans. 1986. *The Bijak of Kabir.* **Delhi: Motilal Banarsidass.**
Perhaps the best published set of translations of the most well-known and powerful bhakti poet. It also includes notes and useful short biographical and interpretative information by Linda Hess.

Ilaiah, Kancha. 1996. *Why I am not a Hindu.* **Kolkata: Samya.**
A provocative declaration by a leading intellectual of the 'Dalit-Bahujan' movement, emphasing the difference in cultural, religious and productive life between the brahman and other 'upper' castes and the masses who are now classified as OBCs and dalits. Ilaiah stresses that the latter are the "productive" and scientific communities of India.

Mani, Braj Ranjan. 2009. *DeBrahmanising History.* **New Delhi: Manohar.**

A useful survey of four thousand years of Indian history, from the perspective of the subaltern anti-caste movement. Braj Ranjan Mani is a well-known journalist, activist and intellectual whose writings concern themselves with the goal of annihilation of caste.

Omvedt, Gail. 2003. *Buddhism in India: Challenging Brahmanism and Caste.* **New Delhi: Sage.**

A survey of 2500 years of Buddhism from an Ambedkarite point of view. It includes a discussion of its background, philosophy, the type of society it fostered; a brief look at the changing forms from Theravada to Mahayana and Vajrayana, and developments in the modern period with Ambedkar's 'navayana Buddhism'.

Phule, Jotirao. 2007. *Slavery.* **New Delhi: Critical Quest Publications.**

'Slavery' is a translation of Phule's first major tract, *Gulamgiri.* It is a hard-hitting satirical account of how the 'avatars' of orthodox Hinduism can be interpreted as stages of the Aryan invasion of India. The Introduction is in Phule's own English and shows that he could, when necessary, write powerfully in this language also. It gives the basis of his thinking. This is taken from the Leftword edition of Phule's work edited by G. P. Deshpande, which also contains Shetkaryaca Asud ('Whipcord of the Cultivator'), where he gives a full analysis of human development up to and including British rule in India.

Zelliot, Eleanor. 2002. *Dr. Ambedkar and the Untouchable Movement.* **New Delhi: Bluemoon Books.**

This is a long-awaited publication of the PhD. dissertation of the most well-known and knowledgeable scholar on Ambedkar. It was probably the most read unpublished dissertation until Bluemoon finally did it. It provides a useful survey of Ambedkar and his movement.

Index

national movement, communists on, 46

National Women's Studies Conference, Calcutta, 85

Naxalism, 73

Naxalite(s), 79
  movement, 75
  organisations, xi
  revolt, 77

Nehru, Jawaharlal, 4, 45, 67, 69, 70, 104
  condemning of caste, 7
  secularism of, 8

Nehru-Mahalanobis planning, 70

'Nehruvian model', of development, 69, 70

Nehruvian secularism, 101

Nehruvian socialists, 6

'new economic policy', of 1990s, 72

Nimbalkar, Waman, 80

Nitish Kumar, 95

non-Brahman movement, 58, 59
  in Bombay and Madras Presidencies, 43
  in Tamil Nadu and Maharashtra, 39–40, 65

Orientalism, 3

'other backward castes'(OBCs), xi, 28

Pakistan, demand for, 58, 63

Pandarpur, Vitthala deity in, 18

Partition, 68

Patel, Sharad, 76

patriarchy, 37
  and caste, 76

Pawar, Sharad, 95

'Periyar', E.V. Ramaswami, xi, 28, 57, 59, 64, 101, 104

anti-caste radicalism of, 61

arrest of, 61

and Congress, 59–60

in Vaikom temple satyagraha, 59

Peshwa, in Maharashtra, 22

Phule, Jotiba, xi, 9, 23, 30, 38, 39, 46, 51, 58, 59, 60, 68, 69, 99, 101, 104, 105
  anti-caste stand of, 26
  'feminist' leanings of, 31
  on Hinduism, 27
  ideology of, 43
  Satyashodhak Samaj of, 24
  as social reformer, 24
  on women, 27

Phukon, Girin, 64

planning, 70
  see also Five Year Plan

Poona Pact (1932), 49

poverty level, population living under, 72

Prarthana Samaj, 24

Priyadas, 19

public sector, 70

Punjab, opposition to Brahman-bania Delhi rule, 87

Punjabi/ Sikh identity, 63

Puranas, 32

Rajadurai, S.V., 59

Rajah, M. C., 65

Rajshekar, V.T., 75

Ram, Mangoo, 58

'Ram raj', of Gandhi, 5, 67, 68

Ramabai, Pandita, 27, 30, 34, 37
  conversion to Christianity, 30–32
  on Hinduism, 32, 35

Ramayana, 39, 85
  image of Sita in, 102–4

Ramdas, in Maharashtra, 19